TOMBSTONES
WITHOUT
A TOMB

KOREA
FOUNDATION

The Korea Foundation has provided financial assistance
for the undertaking of this publication project.

TOMBSTONES WITHOUT A TOMB:
Korea's Queen Sindeok from Goryeo into the Twenty-First Century

Published in 2017 by Seoul Selection U.S.A., Inc.
4199 Campus Drive, Suite 550, Irvine, CA 92612

Phone: 949-509-6584 / Seoul office: 82-2-734-9567
Fax: 949-509-6599 / Seoul office: 82-2-734-9562
Email: hankinseoul@gmail.com
Website: www.seoulselection.com

ISBN: 978-1-62412-102-9   52800
Library of Congress Control Number: 2017957616

Printed in the Republic of Korea

TOMBSTONES WITHOUT A TOMB

Korea's Queen Sindeok from Goryeo into the Twenty-First Century

Hildi Kang

Seoul Selection

For Gari
Mentor and friend

Attentive ghost

Dark silent figure

Standing in the doorway

Of these words.[1]

Contents

Preface and Acknowledgments

"This is the book I wanted to read but couldn't find,
so I wrote it myself."[2]

It began with a photo in the newspaper.

One day in 1994, a Korean newspaper carried a photo showing a tombstone embedded in the wall of a sewer in Seoul and claimed that the stone had come from the tomb of Korea's Queen Sindeok. With this photo, the queen commandeered my life. I determined to learn what had caused her tombstone to be down in the filth of a sewer. I searched for her name in every source of Korean history I could find. At the Center for Korean Studies at the University of California at Berkeley, Clare You, Jonathan Petty, and Ha Yangwon offered me advice, encouragement, and appointment as a research fellow; at the East Asian Library at Berkeley, Bruce Williams, He Jianye, and Chang Jaeyong helped me navigate the various source materials.

I found very little. The few Korean books that did mention this queen seemed to care only of her dishonor in 1400 and her eventual reinstatement in 1669. What happened during all those silent years? Had anyone even thought of her? Why would Song Siyeol suddenly take up her cause in 1669? What happened after the enshrinement? Did she just sink back into oblivion? How did the tombstones get into the sewer? Is there a story here? Is the entire story perhaps more significant than just the single enshrinement day? I needed to find the answers.

Thus I began multiple trips to Korea to visit an array of sites directly related to the queen, and as I gathered material, I came to realize that the dilemma surrounding the queen had resulted directly from the shifting tides of the Neo-Confucian philosophy and the passionate Confucian beliefs of various scholars. To understand the treatment of the queen over the years, one had to look at changes within the monarchy and the relationship between the monarchy and the scholar-officials.

The honors and dishonors given the queen at different times focused on four significant sites: her tomb, the Buddhist temple built specifically in her memory, the royal ancestral shrine, and the tombstones taken from her tomb. My attempts to understand their significance led me to a series of most helpful people.

At the Gyujanggak Institute for Korean Studies in Seoul, staff members including Cheong Eun-kyeong, Pak Heul-suk, Park Sook-hee, and Kang Moon-shik made it possible for us to view and handle—protected by a velvet-covered tray and the use of white gloves—the actual handwritten manual from 1669 that guided the queen's eventual enshrinement at Jongmyo Shrine.

At Chohung Bank in Seoul, Cho Daegyu, team leader of the Miniature Bridge Restoration Project, gave us a copy of a booklet documenting the history and condition of the Gwangtonggyo Bridge—the bridge that used the queen's tombstones for support, and which happened to be underground directly beneath the bank. Mr. Cho also introduced us to the bank's photographer, who offered us a copy of its book on the bridge and gave me a set of detailed photos of the sewer-encased tombstones.

Journalist Yeom Young Nam guided us to the Seoul Metropolitan

Government's Cheonggyecheon Stream restoration project, where we met project team leader Choi Dong-yun and publicity team leader Kim Chang-geon, who supplied us with copies of their research and explained plans to restore the stream as it flowed through central Seoul. They arranged for us to go down into the sewer to see the embedded tombstone, providing a safety team that assured us there was a cement divider separating the actual sewer from our path along a dry (that day) rain runoff section.

Multiple visits to Jeongneung Royal Tomb, the queen's tomb, brought another series of unexpected pleasures. Site directors Ho Yeom-kyu and Kim Yong-uk and staff member Cho Han-geung allowed us carefully, and with restrictions, to climb the burial mound and photograph the stones. The head of maintenance seemed delighted to have visitors who wanted information. He grinned happily as he produced an ancient key, unlocked the wooden lattice door of the small tile-roofed building, and allowed me in to photograph the King Gojong stele honoring the queen.

Our circle expanded. The manager of the tomb site told us of the incense ceremony (*jehyang*) performed every September by descendants of both families (Yi on the king's side and Kang on the queen's) to honor the queen, and we planned our next trip accordingly. Returning to Jeongneung Royal Tomb for the ceremony, I expected to stand in the background and quietly observe the ritual. I forgot, of course, that as a gray-haired Westerner, I could not "blend in" anywhere in Korea. As we turned to leave at the end of the ceremony, one of the elders stopped us, asked why we had come, and insisted that we join their picnic lunch. Yi Yugil and Kang Sinju offered spontaneous friendship, and Yi Sammok, branch head of the Songpa-gu Yi Clan, sent us manuals with details of both the Jongmyo

Shrine and Jeongneung ceremonies. Director Kim Yong-uk sent us information about the management history and current ceremonies of both Jeongneung Royal Tomb and Jongmyo Shrine.

And then we met with the old woman who ran the snack shop just across the creek. We had been told she had an extraordinary story to tell, and I have included it here as an epilogue.

In addition to all of our visits to specific sites, many individuals offered help, advice, and suggestions. Professor of history Yun Jeong-nan and head of exhibits at Deoksugung Palace Museum Lyu Ma-ri each added pieces of missing information. Clark Sorensen and Martina Deuchler each took time to read and comment on early drafts of what was to have been a journal article, and as such was presented at Association of Asian Studies conferences in Phoenix (2004), Chicago (2005), and San Francisco (2006). Many specific questions were graciously asked or answered by Ahn Young-ok, Robert Buswell, Henry Chau, Cho Insoo, Carol Dent, John Duncan, Charlotte Horlyck, Kim Nan, Kim Sunjoo, Lewis Lancaster, Gari Ledyard, Shin Gi Wook, Syn Chol, and Sem Vermeersch.

Finally, special thanks to the people at Seoul Selection for their trust in this book and their work to make it presentable. Thanks to Hank Kim and Jin Lee for accepting the manuscript, and to Park Jiyoung and the editors whose eyes for precise detail found all the errors I so easily overlooked. My thanks to each of you.

The search for Queen Sindeok thus spread out across the years, yet the slowness of the effort allowed time for the resulting volume to include an unanticipated grand finale—the singularly personal honor to the queen that brought her story full circle back into the center of Seoul. The elegant and professionally carved tombstones that first surrounded her tomb and then went from dump heap to sewer—these very stones now grace the retaining wall of the Cheonggyecheon Parkway, inviting every passerby to observe their beauty, wonder at their history, and perhaps even ask the question, "Just why are the tombstones for this queen so far removed from her tomb?"

A Note to the Readers

Romanization of Korean Words and Names

This book follows the revised romanization system for Korean words, except for personal and institutional names for which the individuals and institutions in question have chosen different spellings. For detailed information and pronunciation guidelines, please refer to the website of the National Institute of Korean Language.[3]

Personal Ages

Westerners measure personal ages in years completed. But Korean custom also counts the year in progress; thus a newborn infant is already "one" (that is, in his or her first year). This might be likened to school, where a child is said to be in "first grade" upon entering the classroom. This difference in calculating age often accounts for seeming disagreement among sources—for example, whether a person married at age thirteen (Western) or fourteen (Korean). In this book we will follow the Western custom.

Names of Months

Dates before the 1900s are based on the lunar calendar, which follows the shifting phases of the moon. Thus, months herein are not given the names used in the stationary Western calendar, but are referred to as the lunar "first month," "sixth month," and so on.

INTRODUCTION

Gwangtonggyo bridge was originally built with dirt and wood, but it was destroyed by massive flood. In 1410 (10th year of King Taejong's reign), the bridge was reconstructed using the stones from the tomb of Queen Sindeok (Jeongneung Royal Tomb).

Jeongneung was the first royal tomb built in the Joseon Dynasty, and the quality of its carving, which was produced along with the tomb, is considered the best for a stonework in that era in sophistication and magnificence.

Embedded in the wall of a newly built parkway that cuts through the center of Seoul are tombstones that in 1396 surrounded the tomb of Korea's Queen Sindeok. Why these ornately carved stones are now in public view rather than surrounding their assigned tomb is the final act in a story that covers six hundred years and introduces us in very personal terms to the queen and the men who ruled the Joseon Dynasty—the Neo-Confucian royalty and their scholar-officials. The tombstones present a graphic introduction to this queen and offer a tangible footprint to the entire trajectory of her story. They began in their expected place of honor surrounding her royal tomb, then slid through increasing levels of neglect and abuse until finally they were rediscovered and restored to a new place of public honor. The story of these stones parallels that of the queen.

Queen Sindeok, wife of the founder of Korea's Joseon Dynasty in 1392, was appropriately honored during her life. She had no political power and no reason to be remembered, and if the dynasty's third king had not interfered, perhaps indeed she would have faded from memory. However, through no fault of her own, she became entangled in the extraordinary events that accompanied the dynastic change of 1392 and because of them became severely dishonored after her death.

Aside from the insult of the dislocated tombstones, her spirit tablet was misplaced, her prayer temple was scaled down and moved, and through it all proper rituals were not done—or were done for a time but discontinued. Ironically, to borrow from Kenneth Foote, "the organized forgetting didn't work; the tragedy would not go away."[1]

A Unique Situation

This book challenges the commonly held view that Queen Sindeok's importance was limited only to her dishonor in the 1400s and enshrinement in 1669. Her story—both the slow road to reinstatement and the multiple references to her in the years that followed—was hindered by official fear of acting against royal precedent and by the inordinate display of factional politics. These two points—factional influences and the power of precedents—are the main issues illuminated through the examination of official and unofficial records.

This study also takes issue with the de-emphasis of Queen Sindeok's story, and suggests that the totality of her narrative across the centuries would have been explored and known in detail if it had not been overshadowed by the well-documented factional fights of 1659 and 1674, each filled with vitriolic accusations, forced exiles, and court-ordered suicides. The year of her reinstatement,1669, was a year of relative harmony between factions and the level of agreement would have been noticed and applauded had it not been sandwiched between the two infamous factional fights.

This effort, this digging into the past, thus gathers forgotten remnants one by one and fits them together until they gradually reveal unexpected patterns. Queen Sindeok's story is no exception;

fragments long lost reemerge. (1) Her story identifies four sites in Seoul that figure prominently in the narrative and remain extant and accessible, blending the ancient into the tangible and modern. (2) It highlights the Confucian tenets of proper rituals and the need to follow ancient precedent, each of which bound kings to inaction and defeated the appeals by scholars in the queen's behalf. (3) It suggests that Queen Sindeok's enshrinement in 1669 was not the most important issue. Rather, it was the king's actions, for he broke with not one, but two traditions when, lacking any appropriate precedent, he allowed the ceremony and then allowed scholars to use their own wisdom to create the manual. (4) The queen's story highlights the historical change that followed her enshrinement, when from 1669 onward scholars no longer looked for ancient precedents to honor royal ancestors, but looked directly to Queen Sindeok's manual as the new guide to follow. And, finally, (5) this narrative presents for the first time in English much of the elaborate detail surrounding the enshrinement of the queen's spirit tablet at Jongmyo Shrine, with instructions and drawings found only in the extant manual.

Centuries of a Conundrum

The Queen Sindeok narrative progresses simultaneously on three levels: her personal story, the development of Korean history, and the changes in Confucianism over time. The controversy surrounding the queen rested on an argument that divided the royal court for centuries: the rightful place of this queen, who married in one dynasty and rose to royalty in the next. The problem lay entwined in the severe legal changes that came about as the dynasties changed. For example, in the preceding Goryeo Dynasty (918–1392), multiple wives enjoyed equal status, and the young Queen Sindeok had the misfortune to be married during the Goryeo era as Yi Seonggye's (later King Taejo's) second wife. In the following dynasty, Joseon Dyansty (1392–1910), the new Confucian ruling acknowledged only one legitimate wife and that would have been Yi Seonggye's first wife, Lady Han, even though she had died before the new dynasty began. Thus, depending on which set of laws one recognized, Queen Sindeok was a legitimate second wife or an illegitimate secondary wife. From this conundrum developed the centuries of Neo-Confucian arguments and counterarguments.

The Confucian World

Queen Sindeok's story results in a singular case study of the workings of this Neo-Confucian government, with the delicate balance between scholar-officials and throne. Her story highlights the personalities, voices, and powers of these men who, over centuries, put forth their arguments for and against the queen in what each perceived to be the most "heavenly mandated"—and thus utterly essential—aspect of Confucianism. To understand this predicament foisted upon the memory of Queen Sindeok, we must have at least a cursory understanding of the Neo-Confucian world in which she lived. Her situation could only have occurred within that increasingly strict world, a world that came to Korea directly from China.

Korea's Relationship with China

China is ubiquitous throughout this story, for Korea functioned in a clearly defined hierarchy with China at the top and secondary states ranked by how culturally similar they were to China. Acceptance of this hierarchy placed Koreans in a peripheral and somewhat subservient position, but it also affirmed their membership in the Confucian civilization—a system that ran on a set of formal and informal norms that guided relationships and provided stability.

The Korean monarchy saw this relationship as more than a political arrangement. It symbolized peace and goodwill between the two countries and mutual protection against foreign invasions. More importantly, it created a secure place for the Korean monarchy in the hierarchy of an orderly universe. The arrangement had definite benefits for Koreans, allowing them to pay tribute to China and then go ahead with their own affairs.[2]

Neo-Confucian Law

A voluntary form of Confucianism had been in Korea since the fourth century CE, but in 1392 the Joseon government chose to translate Confucian precepts into Neo-Confucian law for the governance of the new country. During the dynasty this system became the only acceptable Confucian orthodoxy in Korea.

"In Korea," write Janelli and Janelli in *Ancestor Worship*, citing Korea's Ministry of Culture, Sports and Tourism, "Confucianism was accepted so eagerly, and in *so strict a form*, [italics mine] that the Chinese themselves regarded the Korean adherents as more virtuous than themselves and referred to Korea as the country of Eastern decorum, referring to the punctiliousness with which Koreans observed all phases of the doctrinal ritual."[3]

The Korean Monarchy

Each Korean king faced a difficult task—he had to be a learned Confucian, walk a fine line between various constraints, and at the same time cultivate his own power. Three forces curtailed the power of the throne: the mandate of heaven, historical precedent, and the power of the scholar-officials.

The mandate of heaven. The rhetoric of the ideal Confucian kingship proclaimed that, due to the ancestors' virtue, heaven had conferred a mandate upon the ruling family, giving it the responsibility of governing in accordance with heaven's will. The mandate, however, was conditional. A good and virtuous leader would receive heaven's blessing and his kingdom would prosper. On the other hand, heaven would withhold the mandate from a selfish, despotic ruler, leaving his country to fail. No ruler wanted to lose the mandate. Thus, in reviewing the case of Queen Sindeok, a monarch who considered reversing an earlier ruling by one of his ancestors moved with extreme caution, for a former king ruling under the mandate of heaven could not have made a mistake.

Historical precedent. The point of view that dominates this manuscript is the overwhelming need of these scholars to look backward to locate a Chinese precedent, forcing every action to be argued and supported by a similar incident in Chinese history. It is stunning and sobering to witness the stranglehold this imposed on every thought and action. Scholars took great care in their study of Chinese history, for Confucian rule depended on historical precedent, insisting that nothing could be added to or subtracted from the traditional wisdom of the Chinese sage-rulers. Historical knowledge helped one make better decisions and was studied whenever a new social policy had to be devised.

"In fact," writes JaHyun Kim Haboush in *A Heritage of Kings*, "discussions were so strewn with historical analogies, allusions, and debates that one is often reminded of a seminar on history."[4] Thus, when it was impossible to find suitable evidence in the literature, the making of decisions was greatly hampered and at times delayed for years.

Scholar-officials. The Joseon Dynasty had learned men in government leadership roles. Its scholar-officials were required to have extensive knowledge of classical Chinese history and literature before taking the civil service examination. Conflicting opinions exist about these men, for their knowledge and wisdom were often overshadowed by their bickering and power plays. The most reader-friendly explanation is energetically expressed by Bruce Cumings:

> The doctrinaire version of Confucianism dominant during the [Joseon Dynasty] made squabbles between elites particularly nasty. ... The losers often found their persons, their property, their families, and even their graves at risk from victors determined to extirpate their influence—always in the name of a higher morality, even if the conflicts were usually about political power.
>
> With that off the chest, we can also say that few civilizations have ever produced people of higher learning, better moral bearing, or more finely honed integrity than the old fogies of the [Joseon] period. As [missionary and early Korean studies scholar James Scarth] Gale put it, "The more I study them the more I honour the sincerity, the self-denial, the humility, the wisdom, the devotion that was back of the first founders, great priests of the soul." They embodied the venerable principle of superior moral example, and they cast a humbling shadow that carries down to our time.[5]

Spirit Tablets

One component of life in these ancient days that carries across the centuries is the importance of spirit tablets (*sinju*). These tablets figure prominently in the worldview of the Joseon Dynasty and thus we must try to understand both what they are and what they meant to the people of the times.

A spirit tablet can be an elusive concept in the modern, logic-driven world. It looks to be only a small piece of wood, perhaps twelve inches high, with the name of the deceased inscribed on it. But it was more—much more. The intangible world was filled with the spirits of the deceased, as alive in death as they were in life. These spirits might rest peacefully in graves or wander restlessly in the netherworld hoping for proper graves. Wherever the spirit dwelled, it came when called to indwell the spirit tablet. Thus, to the believer, that small piece of wood became the temporary dwelling of the "person" and demanded all attendant respect.

In 1432, the official Hwang Hui requested of King Sejong that people use only wooden tablets, not portraits, to call the spirits, saying, "[A]ncient documents (*Geunsarok*, *Mungonggarye*, and *Samagongseoui*) say that when portraits were copied, the hair and beard may not be exactly the same, and thus you will be performing rituals for a different person."[6] Years later, in 1669, Chief State Councillor Jeong Taehwa questioned whether a spirit actually dwelled at the grave or with the tablet. But whichever the case, everyone understood that once rituals began for a person, that person's spirit claimed the tablet as its residence.[7] Proper care of the spirit tablet was imperative, and it generally stood in a tiny cabinet with doors that were opened only when the spirit was called to attend.

A Lighter, Brighter Side

Queen Sindeok's saga is weighed down by death, dishonor, argument, and indecision, yet entwined with it is a brighter side. Her story teems with drama, action, and movement. It simmers with passion, determination, and ferocity of conviction. A king with passion calls for the most skilled workers to carve tombstones for his wife's tomb. A later king with the courage of his convictions holds out for three years against the verbal pounding of his scholars; and those scholars, equally impassioned, come before the throne one hundred, even two hundred strong. They spoke, acted, and persisted with uncommon zeal for or against the memory of the queen.

The story flows with movement. Temples were moved; graves and tombstones went in different directions. Kings came and went; arguments surfaced and trailed away; royal processions crossed the city with marchers, horses, banners, and trumpets. Officials traveled in search of documents, lost graves, and forgotten home sites. Change is constant.

And then there is color. The entire story takes place in the most colorful of all Korean settings—the royal palace. Cinnabar-red pillars, rose-hued brick walls, rafters painted with designs of green, orange, and yellow fill every building. People rush hither and yon, with men in robes of red, green, yellow, and vibrant blues, eunuchs in green, serving girls in blue, and even police in robes of black, red, yellow. Imagine the colors as the story progresses.

The Search

My search for Queen Sindeok's name in English-language sources proved fruitless and I turned to Korean publications to piece together her story. The ancient texts included the *Goryeosa* (Annals of the Goryeo Dynasty), the *Joseon wangjo sillok* (Annals of Joseon Dynasty), the *Seonwon bogam* (Comprehensive History of the Joseon Dynasty), and Yi Geung-ik's *Yeollyeosil gisul* (Unofficial Records of Joseon Dynasty). "Official" documents were those approved by the throne; "unofficial" writings were the work of private scholars.

Goryeosa. The *Goryeosa* is the official history of the Goryeo Dynasty (918–1392), compiled not during that dynasty but during the early years of the Joseon Dynasty. Although several earlier drafts were written, each proved inadequate and none pleased the king. Expanded and finished in 1451, this version contains annals, monographs, and biographies. Although designed with a slant to justify the 1392 change of dynasty, it remains the fundamental document for the study of Goryeo Dynasty.

Joseon wangjo sillok. The *Joseon wangjo sillok* (hereafter the *Sillok*) is the official history of the Joseon Dynasty. During each king's reign, extensive daily accounts were kept by eight diarists/historians who took turns being at all public functions of the court, recording every action and conversation. At each king's death, these accounts, augmented by other official documents, were edited into one official account.

Four copies of the *Sillok* were made and put in separate archives scattered around the peninsula to ensure preservation from disasters. The closest to Seoul was the archive on Ganghwado Island just west of the capital in what is now Incheon. On several occasions within the Queen Sindeok story, when an important decision required a royal precedent, the historians first needed to obtain special permission to travel to the island's archive and view the relevant sections of the *Sillok* and then report their findings to the king.

To be objective, these voluminous accounts give us a daily look into court life, but it must be noted that they were compiled and edited after a king's death by scholars loyal to their monarch. A certain amount of skepticism may be appropriate.

Seonwon bogam. This document records the pedigree of the Yi family, the royal house of Joseon. Seonwon is the former name of the Deogwon area of Hamgyeong-do, the province where the Yi family first came to fame.

Yeollyeosil gisul. Compiled and written by Yi Geung-ik (pen name Yeollyeosil, 1736–1806) this unofficial history describes events of the Joseon Dynasty, and is one of the most widely circulated histories in Korea. The book contains excerpts from various histories, and the writer clearly credits the sources of the excerpts. He compiled his work in the late 1700s; the volume used for this research is a 1966 reprint.

Recent Korean Sources

Other details of the story were found in the works of Yun (1999) and Im (2003), cataloging queens of the Joseon Dynasty, and in Ji Doo-hwan's writing on King Taejo and his relatives (1999). Brief mention of the queen is made in the *Hanguk minjok munhwa daebaekgwasajeon* (Encyclopedia of Korean Culture, 1991), and even the widely used new edition of Yi Hongjik's *Guksa daesajeon* (Encyclopedia of Korean History, 2002) has only a short entry that offers nothing new, for it is taken directly from the *Seonwon bogam.* Details of current ceremonies at Jongmyo Shrine and the tomb come from documents offered by the Jeonju Yi Clan Office.

Sections of the Book

Queen Sindeok's story falls into four separate parts, each of which reflects the changing environment of the Joseon Dynasty. Parts One and Two are driven by the power of the kings, while in Part Three the focus shifts to the court officials who across centuries stood before their monarchs arguing passionately for the restoration of this queen's honor. Part Four opens with a clear example of factional rigidity and its effect on royal honors. Several of these subjects, especially the enshrinement details and tomb rituals, are unavailable in English, and the variety inherent throughout the story makes it a monograph accessible to diverse readers.

Part One, "Honor (1335–1397)," offers what is known of the queen's early life, her four years in the royal court, her death, and the special efforts made by her husband, King Taejo, to plan and oversee her royal burial.

Part Two, "Dishonor (1398–1450)," describes the two major causes that led to her dishonor, delineates the specific dishonors, and presents the four significant sites that continue to be associated with the dishonors.

Part Three, "Ideological Warfare (1500–1669)," is powered by the unyielding work of court officials as they argue to reinstate elements of the queen's honor. Resolution of this dispute is continually blocked by the need of the Neo-Confucian monarchs to follow ancient precedents, of which none existed. Eventually, in a dramatic turnabout championed by the scholar Song Siyeol and fueled by agreement among factions that had previously been known for their vitriolic arguments, King Hyeonjong in 1669 chose the stronger of two "rights" and ordered a reinstatement ceremony.

Part Four, "A Name Remembered (1674–2005)," picks up after the 1669 restoration of honors, as the queen's name continued to surface, but with a significant change. Her name, so long ignored, now becomes the one held up as the precedent to follow when honoring royalty. However, those very factions that joined forces in 1669 now reveal a different spirit as their disagreements lead to exiles and deaths. Finally, Queen Sindeok enters modern society (1958–2005) as Koreans reclaim their history after the devastation of Japanese colonial rule and the Korean War. The democratically elected government, in taking steps to rectify the past, completes the restoration of Queen Sindeok, her tomb, her rituals, and eventually the dislocated tombstones.

This study presents a comprehensive rendition of Queen Sindeok's story and calls us to acknowledge Lowenthal's admonition that "however voluminous our recountings, we know they are mere glimpses of what was once a whole living realm. The memory of that world is not a bright, shining crystal, but a heap of broken fragments, a few fine flashes of light that break through the darkness."[8]

May this monograph shine such a flash of light onto Korea's Queen Sindeok.

Part One

HONOR

(1335–1397)

Seonjukgyo Bridge is a stone bridge built during the Goryeo Dynasty, located in Gaeseong, North Korea. The bridge is well known as the place where prominent Neo-Confucian scholar-official and statesman Jeong Mongju (1337–1392) was assassinated. Jeong Mongju opposed building a new kingdom, the Joseon Dynasty, and remained loyal to the Goryeo Dynasty. Before the founding of the Joseon Dynasty, Yi Bangwon (later Taejong of Joseon), fifth son of Yi Seonggye, who became the first king of Joseon, killed Jeong Mongju on the Seonjukgyo Bridge.

Chapter 1

THE EMERGENCE OF YI SEONGGYE AND LADY KANG

Yi Seonggye and his second wife, Lady Kang, eased their way into Korean history during the second half of the 1300s. Actions outside of and within the Goryeo Dynasty (918–1392) precipitated Yi's rise from warrior to king, and it is during these tumultuous years that Lady Kang enters the royal records.

Mongol Power

Genghis Khan had led the Mongols to become a major force across Asia, and their eventual presence in Korea set in motion events that brought General Yi and his wife into history. In the early 1200s the Mongols flexed their power in northern China, gradually conquered the area, and in 1271 named their dynasty Yuan (Won in Korean). Yet while they were still fighting in China, they had also been fighting in Korea. Genghis Khan's grandson Kublai flooded troops into Korea and as Mongol armies fought their way down the peninsula multiple times, Koreans pushed back again and again. Finally, just two years after giving name to their new dynasty, the Mongols in 1273 secured their rule in Korea. At that point, Korea chose to submit in order to end the fighting. They paid dearly for the privilege of peace, sending exorbitant tribute to the Mongolian capital of Khanbaliq (near modern-day Beijing), including royal hostages—each crown prince of Korea spent his youth in Khanbaliq where he learned Mongol ways, married a Mongolian bride, and returned to his homeland only when it was his time to rule.

Into this Mongol world Yi Seonggye's family appears.

The Jeonju Yi Lineage: Warriors

Yi Seonggye entered the record in 1335, born into a family living in the northeast area of Yeongheung in the province of Hamgyeong-do. Here the mountains formed a stronghold for Jurchen bandits from across the northern border (today's Manchuria), and the men of the Yi clan developed a reputation for their strength in fighting against these infiltrators. Goryeo's king appointed Seonggye's father, Jachun, as the military commander of this northeast region.[1] His sons followed in his footsteps.

In Seonggye's youth, when he was about sixteen, he married a girl known here as Lady Han of the Anbyeon Han lineage, a local family in this northeast region, and she remained his only wife for the next twenty-some years. Between 1354 and 1369 or thereabouts, these two had six sons. They also had two daughters whose dates of birth are unknown. Several of his sons followed the family tradition, began military careers, and with their personal armies gave support to their father as he rose from a local warrior (third deputy commander or *hogun*, rank 4A˙) to a person of significance in the royal capital (chief councillor in the royal court or *munhasijung*, rank 1B).[2] As his prominence increased, so did his contact with the civil government in the capital city of Gaeseong and the people who surrounded the throne.

The Sincheon Kang Lineage: Scholar-Officials

Twenty-one years after Seonggye's birth, in 1356, Lady Kang joins the story, having been born into a family of scholar-officials living near the capital city in the town of Gokju (later Goksan), where members of the Sincheon Kang family held various positions in the civil government. Lady Kang lived in her natal home long before the days when women were confined to the inner rooms, and this fact allows us to imagine her being out and about, hearing tales that blended the politics of the day with local stories of her own father, uncles, and brothers, and of the increasingly famous General Yi Seonggye.

Even though Korea chafed under the burden of Mongol rule, the thin layer of aristocracy to which Lady Kang belonged enjoyed luxuries both homegrown and imported.

"It had become one of the most sophisticated states of the age," writes Peter Lee in the *Sourcebook of Korean Civilization*.[3] Gaeseong had been the capital since the dynasty's inception in 918, and had grown to a city of some 130,000 people, where the thatched houses of ordinary citizens clustered together, while across town, stalls in the marketplace carried luxuries from Korea's own artisans and from the vast, multinational Mongol system. One can imagine the aristocratic

---

* This in a system of government ranks from the entry level, level 9, up to level 1, with A and B divisions within each.

women wearing gowns of silk and adorning themselves with peacock feathers, bracelets, and earrings that have survived the ages and now reside in the museums of Seoul. Above these market buildings rose the curved tile roofs of palaces, government buildings, pavilions, and some five hundred Buddhist temples. The main palace sat at the foot of a pine-covered mountain in auspicious surroundings, and chances are that the young Lady Kang never imagined this palace would one day be her home.

Lady Kang's family rose to prominence during these years of both luxury and turmoil. Her great-grandfather, grandfather, and father all apparently held low-level government posts, and are all said to have passed the civil service examination (*gwageo*), allowing them to move up into high positions in the government. Her grandfather, Kang Seo, a first deputy commander (*sanghogun*, rank 3A), is mentioned in the royal records for 1332, when he became involved in a fracas between two kings and supported the wrong one. The record says he was imprisoned while some twenty others went into exile. Three months later, however, a messenger arrived from the Yuan capital of Khanbaliq ordering the release of the entire group.[4]

Shortly before Lady Kang was born in 1356, her eldest brother, Deukryong, rose to right senior councillor (*samsausa*, rank 2A)[5] and two more of her close relatives received appointments—brother Sunryong as chief councillor (*chanseongsa*, rank 2A) and uncle Yunchung as director of the state council (*pansamsasa,* rank 1B).[6] It is quite likely that some of the first stories she heard were about her infamous Uncle Yunchung, whose escapades led to his eventual execution.

China Challenges the Yuan Mongols

During the years of Lady Kang's childhood, mainland China struggled with uncertainty as the Mongol rule in northern China weakened and the southern Chinese moved north to push the Mongols out entirely. These divided loyalties were felt with ominous force when the Korean King Gongmin (r. 1351–1374) took an anti-Mongol stance that set him against many of his own people. However, while the matter divided people, campaigns against bandits and pirates continued. Records show that during these years, interaction between the Yi and Kang families increased, for several lists of soldiers show Lady Kang's cousins, Wonbo and Yeong, fighting in campaigns along with Yi Seonggye and his half-brother Wongye.

When Lady Kang was about seven years old, in 1363, a dangerous situation in the Korean capital of Gaeseong accentuated the Kang family's close ties to the throne. Soldiers attempted a palace coup against their anti-Mongol king, but the king fled the palace with one hundred of his faithful officials and servants and took refuge at the home of Lady Kang's brother Deukryong.[7] Thus it appears that Deukryong's house must have been somewhat near the palace, and he and the king must have been on friendly terms, for the king entrusted his life to this brother of Lady Kang. Following this episode, the king rewarded those who had fought to protect him, making them First-Class Meritorious Subjects. Here again, both Yi Seonggye and Kang Yeong (Lady Kang's cousin) are on the list, thrown together this time for awards rather than battles.

Weakening Mongol Influence

The Chinese had by now officially expelled the Mongols from their country and founded the Ming Dynasty in 1368, but Mongol power hung tight in Manchuria and Korea. By 1374 (when Lady Kang was about eighteen), her brother Sunryong received a message saying that the Mongol emperor planned to drive out the anti-Mongol King Gongmin, but the king heard of the message, arrested the pro-Mongol group, and sent Kang Sunryong, along with the respected scholar Jeong Mongju and many others, off for one year's exile. Almost immediately thereafter, King Gongmin died of poisoning and a new king, eleven-year-old U, pardoned the exiles.[8]

During these troubled years, the Yi and Kang families became permanently intertwined.

Chapter 2

SECOND WIFE: GORYEO, 1356–1392

Lady Kang steps into history by offering a cup of cold water to a thirsty general and soon becomes the general's second wife. Later, as the Joseon Dynasty opens, she is given the designation of royal "Illustrious Consort" (Hyeonbi), and finally, shortly after her death in 1396, she is elevated to queen and given the royal name of Sindeok. It begins with a story known to nearly every Korean, the "meeting at the well."

The Meeting at the Well: ca. 1375

One day when the famous General Yi Seonggye went hunting, he became thirsty and stopped at a well in a local village. Seeing a maiden there, he asked her for a cup of water. She scooped up the water, but instead of handing it to him, she first pulled leaves from a nearby willow tree and set them on top of the water to float. Stunned, the general asked why, and the maiden replied, "The general must be very thirsty, and if he were to gulp down the water, it might do him harm. With leaves on top, he will have to drink slowly." The general, impressed by her wisdom, visited her father, Kang Yunseong and asked for the maiden's hand in marriage.[1]

The meeting, fanciful and romantic, legend or fact, was handed down through the centuries so that four hundred years later, in 1799, King Jeongjo presented it before his assembled dignitaries. He maintained that whether this account was recorded in the chronicles of the Goksan district or people had simply passed it along as oral tradition, it remained well known and people in the area could still guide visitors to the place where it had happened—Yongyeon (Dragon Pond) in front of Yongbong (Dragon Peak).

Family Connections

This vignette gives the impression that General Yi stumbled upon a delightful young woman, became enthralled with her beauty and wisdom, and immediately fell in love. Of course that is possible. However, other information builds a more complete picture. In the easygoing lifestyle of the Goryeo Dynasty, before the restrictions of Neo-Confucianism set in, it was quite probable that Lady Kang and Yi Seonggye already knew, or at least knew about, each other. The *Goryeosa* holds many references to Seonggye and his elder half-brother, Yi Wongye, fighting side by side with Lady Kang's cousins Kang Yeong and Wonbo and being awarded Meritorious Elite status at the same time. Surely these comrades-in-arms talked about their families. More importantly, although no date is given, another marriage bound these two families together. Lady Kang's first cousin Kang U married Yi Seonggye's first cousin, the daughter of his uncle Jaheung.[2] All of these connections would have been well known to General Yi and Lady Kang.

The Marriage: ca. 1376

However it happened that General Yi and Lady Kang first met, they followed Goryeo custom when Seonggye took Lady Kang, twenty-one years his junior, as his second wife.[3] They married around 1376, when he was about forty-one and she twenty, for their daughter was born around 1379, followed by sons Bangbeon and Bangseok in 1381 and 1382.

A Scholar's Comment: 1669

In addition to the legendary meeting at the well, an equally plausible story is that Seonggye chose Lady Kang as his wife to enhance his own prestige, linking his military family to the Kang family, which held a great deal of power in the capital's civil government. The Kang men were well known in the capital and appear to have moved in circles close to the throne, while the men in the general's family had been known for their military prowess and had only recently entered the civil government. Seonggye's first recorded civil appointment was after the marriage, when in 1382 he became chief councillor (*chanseongsa,* rank 2A) and his son Bangwon entered the civil government after passing the civil service examination in 1383. Years later, in 1669, the scholar-official Song Siyeol said that Seonggye chose Lady Kang, perhaps "due to the power and influence of the position occupied by the Sincheon Kang clan."[4]

Multiple Wives during Goryeo Times

At the time of this marriage, having more than one wife was a common practice, and second and subsequent wives were equal in status to the first. These families could coexist, for in those days women had their own inheritances and kept their own residences, where they lived together with any young children they had. It is of prime importance to the rest of Lady Kang's story to understand that under Goryeo's law, the status of a second wife was just that—a true second wife in a polygamous marriage, not the concubine of a married man as she would later come to be viewed in the Joseon Dynasty. During the years that followed, this fact was often overlooked or deliberately ignored, and it remained a bone of contention across the centuries.

A prime example of this marriage tradition is found in Yi Seonggye's own family. His father, Jachun, had three wives. Seonggye, as the son of Jachun's second wife, had two half-brothers—an elder brother, Wongye, from his father's first wife and a younger brother, Hwa, from the third wife. Seonggye's position in the middle of this family was of no significance during the Goryeo period, but became a serious problem as the later Joseon Dynasty developed its strong Neo-Confucian voice.

Thus Yi Seonggye had married his first wife, Lady Han, back in the days when they were both young (sixteen and fourteen, respectively, in 1351) and both lived on the east coast. Their family had grown, so that between 1354 and about 1370 they had six sons and two daughters. Next, sometime around 1376 he married Lady Kang and had another daughter and two sons. The record does not say how long Lady Han and her family stayed on the east coast near her natal home, but by 1388 both families show up far from their original homes and each has its own estate in the fertile valley of Pocheon, some thirty miles east of the capital city.

Rebellion: 1388, fifth month, twenty-second day

A crisis in 1388 set the stage for two related and significant episodes— General Yi's first move against the Goryeo Dynasty throne, and an escape story where both Lady Han and Lady Kang were rescued from the chaos set in motion by their husband's insubordination to the king.

In the summer of 1388, General Yi acted in direct defiance of a royal order. Ming China had continued to surge northward against the Mongols, with whom Korea was still allied, and now word arrived that the Ming leaders intended to solidify their position by establishing a commandery to the northeast of Goryeo and annexing that entire territory. Angered by Ming China's plans, the young King U (age twenty-five) launched an expedition against the Chinese, ordering commander-in-chief Choe Yeong to take Yi Seonggye and Jo Minsu as deputy commanders and head north to attack the gathering Chinese army. Yi Seonggye argued with the king, opposing the plan on several counts, but he followed orders and moved his army northward until they arrived at Wihwado Island on the Amnokgang (Yalu) River. At this point the two deputy commanders, deciding it hopeless to fight the strong Chinese army, completely disobeyed orders, refused to attack the Chinese, and turned their troops back toward Gaeseong. When the king heard that a branch of his own army was now headed toward him, he ordered his men to prepare to defend his palace.[5]

General Yi and his army arrived back in Gaeseong, and with their yellow dragon banner flying high, beating drums shaking the earth, and marching feet sending clouds up dust up into the air, they fought their way into the city through the Sunginmun Gate and over the Seonjukgyo Bridge.[6] The king, along with his queen and General

Choe, fled into a garden pavilion, but Yi's soldiers tore down the wall surrounding the pavilion and grabbed Choe. The old general, ever loyal, bowed twice before his king and then faced General Yi,[7] who sent the old general off into exile.

Escape from the Chaos: 1388

Against this background of clashing swords, flying arrows, and screams of soldiers fighting in the palace comes the next clear reference to both Lady Han and Lady Kang, now living on their separate estates in the valley of Pocheon.

There are two versions of this story—the unofficial one told by the scholar Yi Geung-ik, which speaks of the people as they were at the time, and the official government version, which variously uses or omits (at the whim of the royal chroniclers) their later royal designations. It is worth noting that in both tellings of the story, Bangwon cares for the families equally. For the official version, see Appendix 5.

The Unofficial Escape Story

At that time, Lady Han lived at her estate in Jaebyeok-dong, Pocheon, while Lady Kang also lived in Pocheon but at the Cheolhyeon estate. Bangwon (Lady Han's son, twenty-two years old at the time) worked in the capital and held the rank of senior administrator (*jeollijeongnang*, rank 1B). When he heard of the fighting in the palace, he immediately got on his horse and galloped off to Pocheon without even stopping at his own house, only to find that the estate stewards and all the slaves had already fled.

Bangwon quickly rode to pick up the two women, the two Han daughters, and the three Kang children, and with them fled northeast. He personally put them on the horses, and when the horses had to be fed in the stables, he attended to it. The children of Lady Kang, still young at the time (the two sons were six and seven), were with him on this trip. He took them in his arms and put them on their horses. When they ran out of food, farmers along the road gave them food. While on the mountain pass, news came that government officials were chasing them and intended to arrest them, so they rode all night. They did not dare approach any farmhouse along the way for fear of detection, so they slept in fields.

Finally they arrived in Icheon at the house of Han Chung (possibly a relative). Bangwon gathered a hundred strong men to take positions to resist attack. He told the women and children that General Choe Yeong would not come after them, but even if he did, they had nothing to fear. They stayed there seven days, until things in the capital calmed down. Then they returned to their homes.[8]

The Final Kings of Goryeo Dyansty

When General Yi marched his army back from the Amnokgang (Yalu) River he had taken control of military power, and he now usurped political power by removing the young King U from the throne and installing King U's son Chang (age nine). A year later he deposed Chang and installed forty-four-year-old Gongyang on the empty throne, saying this King Gongyang (r. 1389–1392), unlike King U and King Chang, was a true descendant of the Wang royal line, being the legitimate son of the earlier King Gongmin. But having a king from the Wang family did not help the faltering kingdom.

For years, the country had suffered from incompetent rule. No one cared for the poor, and people in the southern provinces had gotten so desperate that they were selling their own children, while others wandered aimlessly, stole, and slaughtered animals that belonged to others.[9] As the chaos continued around them, Yi Seonggye prepared an elaborate banquet for the new king.

A Banquet to Welcome the King: 1389

This next mention of Lady Kang places her in the center of the action, for here the general and his wife are in the palace dining with the king. The *Goryeosa* relates that General Yi and Lady Kang gave an elaborate banquet to entertain the new king, and in return the king rewarded Seonggye with an elegant robe, hat, and horse saddle. Seonggye put on the clothing and bowed low before the king. There is, however, the hint of a subversive plot here, for after the banquet someone unlocked the palace gate to let General Yi and his family out, and the next day the king was furious at that servant![10]

The Children of Yi Seonggye and Lady Kang

About this same time, two of Lady Kang's young children married and married well. Her daughter, thought to be the eldest, married Yi Je, a Goryeo cabinet minister, and the young couple adopted the son of Yi Je's brother. Adopting the son of a male relative was the only acceptable form of adoption at that time, as it kept the paternal bloodline pure.

In 1390 Lady Kang's eldest son, Bangbeon, age ten, married a thirteen-year-old princess whose father was King Gongyang's brother. They apparently had no children. Three years later, 1393, after the dynastic change, Lady Kang's youngest son, twelve-year-old Bangseok, married his first wife, Lady Yu, but she was "returned." A year later he married Lady Sim, age thirteen, the daughter of a high government official, Sim Hyosaeng. The records say that she had a son, but he apparently died in infancy.[11]

The increasing prominence of both the Yi and Kang families is reflected in these marriages, as one daughter-in-law came directly from the royal line and the other from a high official who held various positions both during the Goryeo period and on into the new Joseon Dynasty.

The Death of Lady Han: 1391, ninth month, twenty-third day

The *Goryeosa* tells little about Lady Han, yet does record that she became increasingly ill and Bangwon asked the king's permission to resign his government post to help care for her. The king denied the request. A month later, at age fifty-five, Lady Han went to join her ancestors.[12]

Other references to Lady Han in the *Goryeosa* tell only of her birthplace, marriage, and children, the rescue in 1388, and her death in 1391. During the Joseon period, the *Sillok* adds two details: In 1398 her spirit tablet was moved from tomb to palace, and in 1408 it was moved again from the palace to Jongmyo Shrine. Centuries later, in 1824, we learn that a stele was erected at her birthplace, for the court decided that although she had not lived to experience the new dynasty, she had mothered six sons who later became its princes and kings.[13]

The Growing Importance of Bangwon

General Yi's six sons by Lady Han vividly reflect the divisions within the country. Three faded out of sight—the first son (Bangu) remained loyal to Goryeo Dynasty, the third (Bangui) showed no interest in politics, and the sixth son (Bangyeon) died young, "before he married." Yi's second, fourth, and fifth sons (Banggwa, Banggan, and Bangwon), with various levels of political savvy and passion, continued to help their father and embroiled themselves in various plots and counterplots. Their political power is echoed by their rapid rise within the government.[14] Of all these sons with names bearing the matching syllable "Bang," the fifth son, Bangwon, is the name to remember, as he soon dominates much of Queen Sindeok's story. A trained Confucian scholar, he passed the civil service examination (*gwageo*) in 1382 and 1383 and became both an active warrior and a scholar-official. Courageous, he earned merit by bringing his own private army to fight alongside his father, and during these chaotic years, he entered the civil service and quickly rose through various positions. His early friendship with Lady Kang is acknowledged in several events, yet it was he who later tried to purge the court of her memory. This aggressive side of his personality did not always have his father's approval, as his handling of Jeong Mongju's opposition makes clear.

The Opposition of Jeong Mongju (1337–1392)

General Yi's own rise to power did not have unanimous support. One leader of the opposition was Jeong Mongju, whose final days epitomize the ruthless ambition of Bangwon and bring forth another mention of Lady Kang.

This scholar held no mixed messages. He stood firm as a great Neo-Confucian scholar and was recognized as a true elder statesman. His contemporary Yi Saek said of him, "Even when speaking at random, Mongju says nothing that does not conform to principle," and he exalted Jeong as the founder of Neo-Confucianism in Korea.[15] Although the Yi family recognized Jeong's sincerity and power, and did its best to win him over, it was to no avail. Jeong responded to pressure with a poem still memorized by Korean schoolchildren.

> Though I die a hundred thousand times,
> Even though my bones become dust and clay,
> Whether a soul I have or not,
> This single red heart for my lord shall never change, never!

Ordering Bangwon on an Errand: 1392

Jeong Mongju gathered his supporters and made plans to undermine Yi Seonggye. When Lady Kang heard that Jeong had plotted against her husband, she sent for Bangwon and ordered him to go find his father and have him quickly return home. This demonstrates, it is said, the decisiveness of Lady Kang.[16]

The Assassination

Wanting to get rid of Jeong Mongju's opposition, Bangwon talked earnestly with his father about taking action against Jeong, but Seonggye would not listen. "Do nothing," he said. "Jeong is my mentor. I respect him. Whether we live or die is up to fate."[17]

Driven by passion and ambition, Bangwon ignored his father, joined his henchmen, ambushed Jeong Mongju, and killed him on the Seonjukgyo Bridge in Gaeseong. In their frenzy they cut off his head, hung it from the bridge, and erected a sign that stated, falsely, "He was a traitor against the government officials and put the country into chaos."[18] The assassination is famous. The bridge is remembered to this day.

Bangwon Appeals to Lady Kang: 1392, fourth month

When General Yi learned what his son had done, he was furious and yelled, "Our family is known for loyalty, and here you have betrayed my trust! You have killed a great scholar loyal to the king. How can you say this is good? I want to drink poison and die!"

Bangwon countered, "They tried to harm us. How can you sit still and do nothing? I am a filial son. I did it for the family."

Lady Kang stood beside her husband, saw his anger, and was afraid to open her mouth. Bangwon called out, "Mother, why don't you defend our action to him?" The *Sillok* clearly says *"eomeoni"* (mother), implying closeness between the two. Although she was Bangwon's elder by only twelve years, here he respects her position and begs her aid. She then takes his side. Lady Kang turned to her husband, saying, "You consider yourself a great general! How is it that you've become so easily surprised and afraid about the turn of events?"[19]

From General to King: 1392, seventh month

By the twelfth day of the seventh month, General Yi—"reluctantly," it is said in the *Sillok*, that official record written mainly by those officials loyal to the general—decided to place himself on the throne

Portrait of King Taejo of Joseon, 1872, Jo Jungmuk, Park Gijun, 218 x 156 cm, ink and color on silk, Royal Portrait Museum Korea (www.eojinmuseum.org)

The portrait is a reproduction painted in 1872 (the 9th year of King Gojong's reign) based on the original, which had worn out with old age.

as the new king of Goryeo Dynasty. A few days later, on the sixteenth, Bae Geukryeom and other officials retrieved the Great Seal of office from the safekeeping of the dowager queen and tried to present it to Yi Seonggye. Yi had locked his door and refused to come out. Bae forced the door open, set the royal seal down in front of Yi, and made the appropriate deep bows. Outside, the crowd beat drums and chanted, urging him to accept the seal.

Still Yi refused, saying, "From ancient times, to be a king there should be a heavenly mandate. I have no such virtue, so how can I accept?" But the officials surrounded him and would not leave. The next day, the seventeenth, in front of Suchangmun Gate at the palace in Gaeseong, the officials lined up in a row in order of rank. Yi came, dismounted his horse, and walked to the throne hall, but refused to sit on the throne. Standing next to the throne, he accepted their homage.[20] With that, he asked the officials to return to their jobs.

Chapter 3

ILLUSTRIOUS CONSORT: JOSEON, 1392–1396

Yi Seonggye, known as King Taejo, ascended the throne at Suchanggung Palace in Gaeseong, and with this abrupt change Lady Kang entered an entirely new phase of her life. Overnight she rose to unexpected honor as the wife of a newly minted king, and one can imagine her sense of importance and anticipation as her husband put on the richly embroidered ceremonial robes of royalty. On that day filled with such excitement, she must also have felt apprehension as she clearly realized that her own lofty position rested on the king's immediate choice of a crown prince.

The official records say little about her now, perhaps because these records were later edited by scholar-officials inclined against her, or perhaps because very little is mentioned about any of the queens. She did spend four intense years at court while the king and his officials moved, built, and organized a new capital city in Hanyang (Seoul) and revamped the government around Neo-Confucian guidelines. She died of an unexplained illness four years later.

Anecdotal Records

During Queen Sindeok's life, the official record seldom mentions her, but Yi Geung-ik, the respected historian of the 1700s, offers several vignettes. Yi does not extemporize but carefully cites his sources, and his anecdotes give the flavor of the times by filling in details otherwise lost to history. Here at the beginning of the dynasty, for example, Yi tells us that when reviewing her case in 1581, long after her death, the scholar-officials stood before King Seonjo and declared that Queen Sindeok had been instrumental in helping Taejo start the new dynasty, and that Taejo loved her and gave her great respect.[1] Another unofficial source, the *Kang-ssi seheon* (Kang Clan Summary), says this young queen contributed greatly to the formation of the new dynasty and that it is a "well-established fact" that she used her intelligence to enhance her position.[2] Yi Geung-ik is more specific, saying that Lady Kang worked alongside Jeong Dojeon as they named various places in Hanyang and within the palace. The vision of this young woman side by side with an official of the court seems impossible and improbable until, again, we realize that this happened just days into the new dynasty, when the openness of Goryeo still held sway.

Whether these sources are reliable or mere legend has yet to be determined.

Choosing the Heir Apparent

The choice of a crown prince to secure the succession to the throne loomed as an immediate necessity, as King Taejo was now fifty-seven years old. He may have expected his advisors to suggest one of his adult sons, for three of the sons remained actively at his side, and each had powerful expectations of being rewarded for the emotional and military help given his father. One can almost hear these three brothers (now ages thirty-five, twenty-eight, and twenty-five) making their plans.

The Problem of Succession

Rules for choosing a crown prince had never been explicitly laid down, and much arbitrary discretion remained with each ruling monarch. Thus, to help with this decision, King Taejo called in his officials, Jeong Dojeon, Bae Geukryeom, Jo Jun, and Nam Eun, and they all agreed that when times were peaceful, convention should apply and rulers should install the eldest son whatever his ability. But in troubled times, such as then surrounded them, the most able son and the one most truly deserving should be installed. They encouraged the king to think carefully, knowing that all three Han sons stood waiting, and that each had proven to be both capable and deserving.[3]

Lady Kang Speaks Out

Lady Kang was not a disinterested bystander. It is, in fact, said that she had been listening in the next room as the men advised the king. Clearly she wanted to protect her own position and that of her family by having one of her own sons proclaimed heir to the throne. When she realized the direction the conversation was headed, her distress rose until her cries could be heard by all. The advisors, startled by the intensity, cut short their session with the king and hurried from the court. Later, when called in again, they spoke in whispers for fear of triggering another outburst.[4]

However, after Lady Kang's outburst, the advisors did consider the two youngest sons. At first they objected to either of Lady Kang's sons becoming the crown prince, for they were still children only ten and eleven years old and neither could be thought of as able or deserving. Lady Kang's first son was unruly, crude, and surely not fit to be king. Her second son seemed a bit better, so advisors Jeong, Nam, and Sim recommended that if the king must install one of Lady Kang's sons, he should choose the younger one.[5]

The Unexpected Choice

Then, in a startling move, King Taejo crossed off all three of his adult sons and chose as crown prince Lady Kang's ten-year-old Bangseok, ignoring both the birth order and the merit of the sons who had helped him rise to power.

Speculation abounds concerning this decision. If the king had appointed by birth order, the choice pointed to the second son. If the deciding factors had been ability and ambition, his fifth son, Bangwon, might have come out ahead, for he was well educated, politically astute, and surely ambitious. Seong Nak-hun posits that King Taejo may have hesitated to appoint Bangwon in spite of his obvious qualities, considering him too headstrong and remembering that he had taken it upon himself to assassinate Jeong Mongju against King Taejo's own clearly stated wishes.[6] And perhaps Lady Kang's passion did prove a tipping point. The *Sincheon Kang-ssi daedongbo* (Comprehensive Lineage of Sincheon Kang Clan) claims the choice was logical because this eighth son was the child of the king's only living wife.

Jeong Dojeon (1342-1398)

At this point, another major scholar, Jeong Dojeon, taking a stance opposite from that of Jeong Mongju, staked his life on the new Neo-Confucian government and the new royal family. He aligned himself with Yi Seonggye, Lady Kang, and the crown prince and remained loyal until his death in the palace coup of 1398. He began as a military advisor to General Yi and stayed loyal in developing the new government. His knowledge and energy aimed at building a Confucian society show in his many writings, in which he developed an administrative code, planned a national education system, and spoke out against the excesses of Buddhism.[7] He may have backed the youngest prince thinking him malleable and young enough to groom for his own purposes. It is true that he quickly became the boy's official tutor, perhaps hoping to protect him from inevitable palace intrigues and also to indoctrinate him into Confucian thought and behavior.

The Destruction of an Alliance

Whatever the reasons, from the moment that young Bangseok rose to be crown prince, any cooperation between Lady Han's three sons and Lady Kang doubtless slammed to a halt. Every story that survives of their earlier lives indicates respect and support between the two families, but with the appointment of Lady Kang's son as the heir apparent, the situation shifted. Surprise and resentment must have flared and then festered as the king's older sons watched Lady Kang and the young prince receiving the honor and attention they felt rightfully belonged to them.

Such resentment doubtless played a role in the dishonors that

Bangwon later heaped upon Sindeok's memory, but right here is the place to tackle an oft-repeated phrase that contains two significant misconceptions: Bangwon hated his stepmother.

Under Goryeo law, Yi Seonggye had two wives and maintained separate households. Lady Kang held no relationship at all to Bangwon; she was simply his father's other wife, with no connection to Lady Han or to any of the Han sons.

The written record points not to any personal hatred of Bangwon for Lady Kang or her sons, but rather to his overwhelming need to retrieve the throne that had slipped out of his grasp and claim it for himself and his family. Securing the throne became his obsession, yet on this day of jubilant announcements, his personal shock would have to be kept subdued.

Officials, also stunned by the choice, quickly moved to deflect the simmering anger. The King Sejong Memorial Society says that, hoping to circumvent trouble, the courtiers loyal to the newly appointed crown prince sent the three Han sons to areas far from Gaeseong to disperse their power.[8] This plan, attributed to Jeong Dojeon, Nam Eun, and Sim Hyosaeng (father-in-law to the crown prince), involved the common ploy of sending unwanted people far into the country. The story looms as an indication of the plots and counterplots that swirled through the royal halls.

Royal Honors

In addition to dealing with all the normal affairs of state, officials made time to bestow titles on each branch of the new royal family. The very day after the formation of the new dynasty, on the eighteenth day of the seventh month of 1392, Lady Han, though deceased, received the posthumous title of Jeolbi (Faithful Consort); two weeks later, Lady Kang received both the formal title of Hyeonbi (Illustrious Consort) and the informal title of Lady Kang (Kangbi).[9] Early the following year (the third month of 1393), in keeping with tradition, appropriate honors went to three prior generations of the families of both Lady Kang and Lady Han.[10]

Later that year, in the ninth month of 1393, Lady Kang's hometown of Gokju was elevated in status and renamed Goksan. With that, her relatives broke off their original connection to the Sincheon Kang lineage and began their own branch lineage, Goksan Kang, in honor of this daughter born in the town of Goksan.

The Dynasty Continued to Evolve

Eleven days into King Taejo's reign, on the twenty-eighth day of the seventh month of 1392, the king sent an emissary to the Hongwu emperor of China to notify him of the dynastic change and the decision to keep the name of Goryeo Dynasty. The emperor sent back an order for King Taejo to come up with a new name. The committee chose Joseon (Morning Calm) and Hwaryeong (Peace and Tranquility) and sent these back to China.[11] The emperor approved Joseon, the envoy returned to Korea with the news, and the people held a grand celebration in honor of the new name.

Within a month, King Taejo ordered that the court move the capital away from Gaeseong as a visual and practical severing of ties with Goryeo Dyansty, yet it took two years to finalize the plan. Eventually they chose Hanyang (Seoul), an area that had been used one way or another since prehistoric times. As a proper royal city, it had the correct geomantic layout for the new palace—mountains to the rear and a river in front—so in 1394 King Taejo sent officials ahead with thousands of laborers to repair and develop the entire city—the palace, ancestral shrine, ministry offices, metropolitan facilities, market, residences, and roads. The city wall alone kept 120,000 men occupied.[12]

Gyeongbokgung Palace received the most detailed overhaul. It sprawled over acres of land with a labyrinth of long, low tile-roofed structures rising on stone foundations—libraries, reading rooms, audience halls, living quarters, kitchens, stables, servants' quarters— all connected by corridors with heavy tiled roofs curved gently at each corner, creating what some have called the "roofs that smile." Scattered among the buildings were pavilions, ponds, and island gardens, all bringing the countryside within the palace walls.

Illness

The next mention of the Illustrious Consort comes six months later, saying that while King Taejo was on a trip, she became ill.[13]

Jongmyo Shrine
Queen Sindeok's First Significant Site

King Taejo commissioned immediate work on Jongmyo Shrine, the royal ancestral shrine and the most important of all Confucian shrines, to ensure a place to install the royal spirit tablets and do proper rituals for each succeeding monarch. As a shrine, it differs markedly from the palace. It has no pavilions or flowering plants; instead, its beauty comes from the surrounding woods filled with locust, oak, pine, willow, and maple trees. The main building stretches long and narrow, with vermillion pillars and gray roof tiles, presenting a dignified, solemn atmosphere. Cubicles line the building, with each prepared to house the spirit tablet of a deceased king and that of his queen consort. King Taejo began this pattern by taking the spirit tablets of four generations of his immediate ancestors from Gaeseong and enshrining them there in a smaller adjacent building, where rituals were held five times each year.

Within a few years this shrine would become one of the sites contributing to the dishonor of Queen Sindeok. Yet in the giddy days of the new capital, no one anticipated such a turn of events.

Chapter 4

QUEEN SINDEOK: JOSEON, 1396–1397

Four years and one month after being named the king's Illustrious Consort, Lady Kang's rise to honor ended in illness and death. First recorded in 1393, her illness became critical in the eighth month of 1396, and palace servants, knowing that death was near, moved her out of the palace to the home of Yi Deukbun, chief administrator for the women's quarters. This common practice avoided leaving any ghosts behind to roam the palace.

King Taejo visited her on the twelfth day of that month, and the very next day she died. His majesty cried aloud and in his grief canceled his morning meetings and, as was the custom, closed the court and all markets for the next ten days.[1] The following day, the crown prince and other officials took off their colorful garb, put on coarse hemp garments, and began preparations for the funeral service. Servants dressed Lady Kang's body with clothes, covered it with a shroud and a quilt, and finally wrapped it with rope.

This royal death—the first in the new dynasty—now precipitated three simultaneous necessities: a funeral had to be planned, a tomb built, and a temple erected where monks could offer prayers to ensure the soul's safe journey.

The Official Mourner

Meritorious Subjects Jo Jun, Kim Sahyeong, and others, in the flowery rhetoric of the day, recommended to the king,

> We believe that Your Majesty, under the heavenly mandate and the loyalty of the populace, has founded the new nation, and this is a result of your deep and perfect virtue. And also, Hyeonbi (Lady Kang) was chaste and her manner of discreet behavior was prudent, disciplined, and self controlled. When peace reigned, she was watchful. In crisis, she participated actively in formulating responses to resolve the crisis. We cannot say enough about her contribution. Now heaven suddenly does not care about her, ending her life, and our sadness is ten thousand times normal . . . You are king and we are your subjects, but on the basis of your grace, you and the queen were like parents to us. Even if our bodies were ground into powder, it would never repay your goodness to us.
>
> We request, therefore, that you should approve one of your Meritorious Subjects to attend the tomb for three years. And from here on, forever, let this become a precedent and for many generations to observe the practice. We humbly implore that Your Majesty accede to our humble request.[2]

The king granted their request and appointed Yi Seo to attend the royal tomb for the next three years.

Battle over Posthumous Titles: 1396, eighth month, twenty-eighth day

The Office of Royal Rituals and Posthumous Titles, Bongsangsi, had the responsibility of choosing posthumous titles for Lady Kang and also for a certain Jeong Huigye, who had died at about the same time.

The officials proffered three suggestions for each person and sent these recommendations up the official ladder to the minister, who sent them to the chief state councillor, who drafted a document and sent it up to the king.[3]

The king took one look at the titles suggested for Jeong Huigye and unleashed his fury. He declared them insulting, condescending, and completely unacceptable. This same man, he said, only a few years earlier had acted along with Nam Eun to force King Gongyang's resignation and open the way for a new dynasty. For this he had been honored as a Meritorious Subject. Remembering this, the king summoned the Bongsangsi official Choe Gyeon and demanded an explanation, asking why the committee had emphasized only Jeong's misdeeds, ignoring his good points.

For being so extremely unfair to Jeong, the official Choe Gyeon went to prison, and the Board of Punishment quickly sent a recommendation that he be executed. Jo Jun, always near the king, came to Choe Gyeon's defense and begged for a lesser punishment— allowing the prisoner to live, but to suffer through one hundred lashes and then be sent into exile. The other officials went to prison and later into exile because they had agreed with their leader and had not questioned him.

Finally, Queen Sindeok:
1396, ninth month, twenty-eighth day

The officials returned to their task, chose new names, and one month later received approval. Jeong Huigye became Lord Yanggyeong (Breathtaking Vista). There is no mention of the king being angered by the previous names suggested for Lady Kang; however, he did not accept any of them. This time she was offered the title by which she is known, Queen Sindeok (or Sindeok Wanghu, "Wanghu" indicating a posthumous name). They named her tomb Jeongneung—the syllable *neung* designates the tomb of a king or queen.[4]

The Eulogy

The king next asked Gwon Geun, the faithful and thoughtful official, to plan the eulogy, saying, "Before I became king, the present queen's help was invaluable. Now, suddenly, with her death, there is no one to give me honest advice by giving me warnings and criticizing my conduct. I am truly saddened. Would you, my minister, compose a eulogy (*jemun*) for her?"

Gwon made many deep bows and said that from time immemorial, when a king received the heavenly mandate and started a new dynasty, without exception he had a capable and helpful spouse. For example, Yu the Great of Xia Dynasty had Lady Tushan, King Tang of Shang Dynasty had Lady Youshen, and King Wen of Zhou had Tai Si, and these emperors were still remembered for their helpful spouses. It was so recorded in history books.

> Our Queen Sindeok was beautiful and intelligent … She was not given to excess … observed proper behavior … was diligent … assisted the king … helped establish a new nation to last for ten thousand generations … and was equal to all other wise queens of history."
>
> Eulogy (in part) written by Gwon Geun[5]

The Royal Funeral

At the beginning of the year 1397, hundreds of officials forsook their colorful robes and put on white robes of mourning to attend Queen Sindeok's funeral.[6] As the first royal funeral in the new capital, it must have been conducted in the tradition carried over from Goryeo Dynasty. In the *Sillok*, Goryeo burial proceedings were described as extremely elaborate, and the mention of "funeral rites" would have included all rites performed before, during, and after the burial, but it seems no details of such ceremonies have survived.[7, 8] However, one list from a later royal funeral specified a procedure: Do not eat, bathe, put on funeral garb, wait, sit in front of spirit tablets, and place the body in the casket. After a proclamation, eulogy, presentation of food and burning of incense, move to the grave site. The ceremony at the grave site must include wailing, a horse ridden, a horse unridden, a red swallow flag, and a white folding screen. At the grave, burn incense again, sing, chant, hold "open the ground" ceremony, pray to the spirit of the mountain. Finish by hanging a banner, putting on cotton shoes, and lighting a candle.

Following the prolonged public ceremony, the king went to Gyeongcheonsa Temple and privately prayed for the spirit of Queen Sindeok—and here perhaps one glimpses not the king, but the private man, craving solitude and simplicity to weep alone in his grief.

The Spirit Tablet's Resting Place

With the burial completed, officials chose Inanjeon Hall in Gyeongbokgung Palace for the temporary resting place of Sindeok's spirit tablet. They returned to the palace with her chestnut wood spirit tablet (*sinju/wipae*) and continued the rituals with a "spirit returning" (*banhon*) ceremony. At this point, since Queen Sindeok had been King Taejo's only living wife and mother of the heir apparent, it was expected that her tablet would rest there until the death of her husband, King Taejo, and then the two spirit tablets would be placed together in their assigned cubicle in the royal ancestral shrine. That was the plan.

Condolences from China's Hongwu Emperor

Following the ceremony, Gwon Geun traveled to China to inform the Ming emperor of the queen's death. When Gwon returned two months later, he brought a letter of condolence that included several of the emperor's own poems and numerous pieces of advice.[9] The letter said, in part:

> I learned from the emissary that the king's [your] first queen, Lady Kang, has passed away. [Lady Han had died before this dynasty began and was not elevated to queen status until 1398. Lady Kang had been crowned in 1396, making her, as the emperor wrote, the "first queen."] Oh, such misery! I'm sure morning and evening you miss her. Why wouldn't you miss her! Isn't Lady Kang the one who supported you when the new dynasty was formed in your country, as the Mother of the Country?
>
> Now this person has disappeared and leaves only a trace. Is it not hard to endure! When she was alive, and in the morning you were dressing for the day, she took time and helped you. And when you were too busy attending affairs of state, too busy to have meals on time, then she would accommodate such delays … When the sun set and darkness came, Lady Kang must have ordered the candles be lit. Now Lady Kang is gone forever … All around you now are only

courtesans and servants.

You touch the coffin with long sighs. How sorrowful. When Lady Kang's spirit looks back from its vantage point, she must feel sorry for you in your loneliness. Now you must look out for yourself. That is why I am sending this condolence.

Following the letter came the emperor's long poems, and after the poems came items of advice. Among them:

- As a small country [you] serving a big country [China] the small one must be honest and sincere.
- There can be only one sun [me]. Do not regard this lightly. Never underestimate the sun.
- Send me only emissaries that can speak Chinese. I am sending Gwon Geun back to you; the others I am keeping. [with no explanation included]

In spite of this courtly rhetoric, the emperor did not grant his gold seal of formal recognition to the new dynasty for eight more years.[10]

The Tomb

While the other preparations were being made, officials began their search for an auspicious tomb site, and the king, dressed in traditional white mourning clothes, set out with his retinue to inspect the proposed sites. They visited Haengju, slightly northwest of the capital, and there the officials argued among themselves so vehemently that the king lost patience and had them whipped! Next they went to Anam-dong, just northeast of the Dongdaemun Gate (Great Eastern Gate), but when they dug into the ground, water gushed out and eliminated that choice. Finally they chose Chwihyeonbang, directly southwest of the palace along the side of Taepyeongno, the main boulevard leading from Gyeongbokgung Palace down to the Namdaemun Gate (Great South Gate). Here, according to the king's wishes, the tomb would be built, putting it squarely in the middle of the city—a strange place for a tomb, some said. No other tomb had ever occupied such a central place. Others said King Taejo had her tomb placed close to his palace so that he could see it daily, but if so, one wonders why he first examined the two more distant sites.

For Confucians, the importance of a proper burial cannot be overstated, and in Sindeok's case, King Taejo himself commissioned and watched over the building of the tomb. The stone wall behind it, the guardian stones beside and in front, the mound itself, and all the attendant rituals were done under the care of King Taejo, but each reenters the queen's story multiple times across the centuries.

The Confucian care for the dead at the grave, as well as in the ancestral hall, was believed to emanate spontaneously from the most natural of all human feelings, filial piety.[11] A properly prepared grave preserved the link between the living and the dead and ensured the well-being of both. If the ancestors found peace in the ground, their descendants would find peace in the world. The *Analects* of Confucius put it this way: The Master said, "[W]hen your parents are alive, serve them in accordance with propriety; when they die, bury them with propriety; and offer sacrifices to them with propriety." Other translations say "in accordance with the rituals."[12]

Because Queen Sindeok's tomb was the first to be built in the Joseon Dynasty, it followed the style of Goryeo Dynasty, with a stone lantern and table exactly like those of King Gongmin (r. 1351–1374). Every mention of the queen's tomb includes the same elusive phrase "in the style of Goryeo," without explaining that style or how it differed from the Joseon style. However, a small booklet, *Royal Tombs of Joseon*, has a picture and description of each royal tomb from the Joseon Dynasty, and observation of the lanterns in each photo supplies the answer.[13] In front of Queen Sindeok's tomb stands the Goryeo-style lantern carved in simple, unadorned lines. By contrast, each of the subsequent Joseon-style tombs has a lantern carved in an elaborate pattern with an ornately carved roof, or capstone.

Stone lantern of Jeongneung Royal Tomb (left)
Stone lantern of Yungneung Royal Tomb built in 1762 (38th year of King Yeongjo) (right)

Tombstones

The tombstones that once surrounded Queen Sindeok's grave mound experienced a journey that echoes that of the queen, moving from honor to the depths of dishonor and then back to a respected and very public place of honor. Because of that parallel fate, they serve as "bookends" to the queen's story, both opening and closing it. With that in mind, one must understand more fully their appearance and purpose.

King Taejo envisioned a great tomb for his wife and he refused to leave anything to chance. He commissioned the governor of Jejudo Island, Yeo Uison, to travel to the capital and supervise a crew of master stonemasons as they carved intricate designs on the massive stones chosen to surround her tomb. These stones are not tombstones in the Western sense but rather huge slabs of granite, sometimes called "hedge stones," which encircle the base of a royal burial mound like a stone hedge.

The stonemasons did their work well. Of the several sets of stones necessary to guard and protect the tomb, the twelve spirit general stones (*sinjangseok*) were acknowledged as masterpieces in their day. They stood three feet high and six feet four inches long. In the center of each stone slab stood the carving of the guardian spirit with both hands clasped, surrounded by a swirling pattern of intricate clouds.[14] One stone has been found carved with a Buddhist lotus-blossom pattern, perhaps a pedestal for a spirit general.

Although the master carvers had been specially chosen to perform that work, their names are unknown, at least in part because of the Confucian prejudice against manual labor, which was perceived as unfit for educated men. Governor Yeo, however, returned home to Jejudo Island with gifts of silk and thirty *seok* of rice (one *seok* equals five bushels) for his mother, showing the appreciation of the king.[15]

The Area Surrounding the Tomb

It is useful now to envision the entire area surrounding the tomb mound in preparation for the repeated problems that surface there in the future. The area is open and parklike, with enough space to house the buildings necessary for proper rituals. One enters the "sacred" area under the freestanding Hongsalmun Gate topped by red arrow-like ornaments, beyond which are stone bridges and a T-shaped shrine. Buildings on either side of the shrine hold a kitchen for preparing ritual foods and a small pavilion for housing a monument, usually a tall stone stele with formal inscriptions carved on one or both sides. The tomb and the mound that covers it sit up on a small hill above the buildings.

Ancestral ceremony at
Queen Sindeok's tomb (top)
Hongsalmun Gate (bottom)

Queen Sindeok's tomb

The hedge stones encircle it, and beside it stand stone guardian sheep and tigers. In front stand one or two pairs of civil officials, and a little farther away stands a pair of military officials. Human guards and caretakers must be assigned to keep the mound free of weeds and the surrounding area free of looters and wild animals.

Queen Sindeok's tomb in the center of the city began with all these appropriate accoutrements and ceremonies.

Heungcheonsa Temple
(Rise to Heaven Buddhist Temple)

In keeping with his Buddhist faith, King Taejo ordered a Buddhist temple constructed just to the east of the tomb. It was a *Wondeok* temple, which means that the monks were commissioned to pray specifically for the departed soul of Queen Sindeok.[16] In the first month of 1397, workmen began digging the foundation, and by the eighth month they had completed the main building.

It is said that the temple had been positioned directly in the center of the city so that the grieving king could hear the reverberations of the mammoth drum and the great bronze bell as they rang out across the valley and echoed off the surrounding mountains sending their prayers to heaven. A poetic story, handed down through the centuries and told again to King Hyeonjong in 1669, expressed how deeply King Taejo felt the loss of his queen. In his affection and sorrow, he refused to pick up his utensils to eat until he heard the temple drum assuring him that the monks were offering prayers for the spirit of his beloved queen.[17] This story presupposes that at least some of the monks had moved onto the temple grounds and begun their rituals soon after Queen Sindeok's death, not waiting for the completion of the temple.

Building the Temple

Heungcheonsa Temple, built to house 140 monks, displays the restrained elegance of traditional Korean architecture. It is a collection of single-story buildings each capped by a heavy tile roof supported by deep-red pillars, with eaves and rafters painted in the colorful patterns of Buddhist symbolism. One must pass through the first gate and then the gate of the Four Heavenly Kings and enter the public courtyard surrounded by a lecture hall, a hall for the main Buddha, a pagoda, a drum tower, and a pavilion to house a great bronze bell. Within the courtyard, workers placed a five-storied pagoda called a *sarira* hall (*sarijeon*) specifically to commemorate Queen Sindeok's death. It was the only *sarira* hall in the country that remained from ancient Silla times (668–936 CE), and it had come from a temple in the Busan area near the village of Mulgeum. Inside this pagoda reposed bones (*sarira*) and Buddhist scriptures.[18] *Sarira* are not truly bones, but a fired substance, tiny glass-like beads left after cremation. A monk, as an enlightened being, would have many of these *sarira* as an indication of his holiness. The *sarira* can be found only by digging in the cremation ashes.

This huge temple had forty-two statues of the royal family's bodhisattva, Bodhisattva Avalokitesvara of Mount Putuo Island in the sea near Shanghai.[19] When Koreans sailed to China, they looked to this mountain as a landmark. The bodhisattva had appeared on that mountain, and having one thousand arms and one thousand eyes, she could be most generous and helpful. The Yi family had chosen this bodhisattva as their own prayer Buddha and thus had included the statues to aid Queen Sindeok's spirit.[20]

In these first few years of the new dynasty, in the very center of the new capital, three out of four sites came into existence that defined the saga of Queen Sindeok: the Jongmyo Shrine (royal ancestral shrine), her royal tomb, and a Buddhist temple dedicated to her spirit. Built to convey honor, each variously and repeatedly dealt dishonor.

Part Two

DISHONOR

(1398–1450)

Injeongjeon Hall in Changdeokgung Palace

Chapter 5

THE CHESS MASTER

Bangwon played a masterful game of chess. He planned, anticipated, set up his moves, and outmaneuvered opponents. His chess board was life; his chessmen, people. He moved off the playing field those who got in his way and he shifted others into line ready for his next premeditated move. Much, but not all, of his maneuvering impacted Queen Sindeok.

It was with Bangwon that the dishonors began.

Later as King Taejong, it was Bangwon who orchestrated the myriad dishonors against Queen Sindeok's memory, and in spite of the widely held perception that he started this chain of events out of vengeance against this one woman, the overarching view shows that he took aim at everyone who stood in his path to secure the throne for a clear and unmistakable line of succession.

The Palace Coup:
1398, eighth month, twenty-sixth day

Queen Sindeok's death in 1396 left her two sons, the young crown prince and his brother, in frightfully weakened positions, and as the new royal family worked to secure the throne, disaster loomed.

When Jeong Dojeon urged the king to disarm all private armies and form a united government militia, Bangwon knew it was time to act.

Resentment erupted into bloodshed. Bangwon called up his men and those of Yi Sukbeon and others, and publicly charged Jeong Dojeon (tutor to the crown prince), Nam Eun, and Sim Hyosaeng (father-in-law to the crown prince) with conspiracy to murder the sons of Lady Han. Bangwon ordered these men to the palace to attend King Taejo at his sickbed and sent soldiers to present the summons. The soldiers found Nam and Jeong drinking wine in the inner chamber of Nam's concubine—surely fortifying themselves for what they sensed was to come. Soldiers entered. Swords flashed. The loyal scholars' lives were over.

Soldiers then went after the two Kang princes (often referred to as the "young" princes, but by now sixteen and seventeen years old) and ordered them out of the palace and into exile. As they traveled, henchmen slaughtered them both. Not satisfied with killing the scholars and princes, soldiers sought out and killed Yi Je (husband of the Kang princess), along with more of their supporters, raising the death toll both inside and out of the palace.[1]

Relatives of the Queen

The terror of a palace coup is never confined to the palace. Thus it is not surprising that the Sincheon Kang lineage record relates that following this coup, relatives of Queen Sindeok fled from the court to escape being connected to the queen and her sons. However, the index to the *Taejo sillok* (Annals of King Taejo) reveals no sign of anyone running away and, in fact, most suffered only short-term confinement, while two brothers and a nephew quickly returned to government service. Queen Sindeok's widowed daughter entered a convent a year later, on the tenth day of the ninth month of 1399 and lived there until 1407. She and her husband had adopted Yi Yun, the son of Je's brother, and this son survived the coup and eventually had six sons and two daughters of his own. Thus, in spite of the murder of Sindeok's sons (and with that, the end of her direct male-line descendants), this adopted grandson's family gave her countless descendants through her daughter.

Royal Turnarounds

Immediately following the coup, Bangwon urged his older brother, Banggwa, to accept the position of crown prince, as this brother was legally first in line for the throne. Later events confirm that Bangwon saw himself as next in line, but dared not demand it, for he had used "hierarchy of age" to justify getting rid of the young crown prince.

Next, King Taejo, filled with grief and discouraged by the chaos that had escalated around him, announced his decision to abdicate the throne, thus adding to the confusion. He moved into Gwangmyeongsa Temple, and writing to his faithful official Gwon Geun he said, "I have with the assistance ... of my ancestors and the hidden aid of Buddha founded this dynasty. I am now too worn out for diligent effort and have put off the heavy burden, wishing only to devote myself entirely to the service of Buddha, prostrating myself before him morning and night."[2]

King Taejo's abdication gave the new crown prince only two weeks to negotiate his rise from prince to crown prince to king, as he replaced his father and became King Jeongjong, the second king of Joseon Dynasty.

One of the first orders of the new king was to return the capital to Gaeseong, where it remained until the following king moved it again back to Seoul. This change makes it somewhat difficult to determine whether the next set of actions occurred in Seoul (Hanyang) or slightly north in Gaeseong.

Queen Sindeok's First Dishonor: A Foreshadowing

King Jeongjong took the throne on the third day of the ninth month of 1398 and began immediately to shift honor away from Queen Sindeok and onto his own mother, Lady Han. With one small move, he cleared the way for Queen Sindeok's single most devastating Confucian dishonor—exclusion from Jongmyo Shrine. Five days after his ascension he ordered Queen Sindeok's portrait scroll (*yeongjeong*) taken out of its designated place in the (Hanyang) palace's Inanjeon Hall and moved to her tomb, where it lay forgotten.

Honors for Lady Han continued. Two weeks later, King Jeongjong held a memorial funeral ceremony for her, as she had died eight years earlier and never been posthumously brought into the new dynasty. Two months after that he elevated her from consort (Jeolbi) to queen (Sinui Wanghu) and designated Insojeon Hall in the Gaeseong palace as her spirit's resting place.[3] Finally, six weeks later her new spirit portrait (*hwasang*) was installed there and the king personally went to perform the rituals.[4]

All these honors for Lady Han took place during the first four months of King Jeongjong's short reign, and what Duncan says about the politics of that time might also be said about the two queens: "It all began right after King Taejong [using Bangwon's later royal name] was formally designated heir apparent, leaving little doubt that King

Taejong was the real mastermind from the very beginning."[5]

Looking at these four months again, the ominous significance for Queen Sindeok becomes clear. Of course Bangwon was the mastermind. An undisputed Confucian scholar, he anticipated how the laws would change and was able to lay the groundwork for his mother's enshrinement at Jongmyo Shrine alongside King Taejo, keeping Queen Sindeok out. Surely he was thinking ahead to the inevitable death of his father, when the retired king's spirit tablet and that of his queen would be enshrined together. Queen Sindeok's spirit tablet had been resting in the palace hall where it had been placed under the guidance of her own husband. Moving Queen Sinui's spirit into the palace and taking Sindeok's out meant that the latter's tablet was no longer in line for Jongmyo Shrine.

Jongmyo Shrine corridor

Bangwon Clears His Path to the Throne

With Bangwon's second-eldest brother now the king, Bangwon knew that any opposition to his own rise to the throne came from only two points—the sons of this brother now on the throne and Bangwon's own fourth-eldest brother. In what became known as the "Second Strife of Princes," Bangwon challenged that fourth brother to a fight on the streets of Gaeseong, won the battle, and eliminated that source of opposition. The brother on the throne, however, had fifteen sons.

Again, Bangwon had preempted the situation. He knew that under the emerging Confucian guidelines, this brother could not pass the crown to any of his sons because none were legitimate; they all came from various now-lesser wives and the new laws shoved them out of the running. The king's first, and thus only legitimate, wife had no children.

Bangwon could now feel free to elevate himself into position as the new crown prince, which he did in the second month of 1400, and nine months later King Jeongjong abdicated in favor of this younger, experienced, and utterly ambitious brother. Bangwon achieved his goal in the eleventh month of 1400, becoming the third king of Joseon—King Taejong.

King Taejong Moves to the Fore: 1400s

King Taejong served as a strong and capable monarch, and his long rule (1400–1418) clearly defined and firmly solidified the dynasty. His strength built a system that lasted more than five hundred years, and throughout his reign he proved himself well spoken, well read, pragmatic, and practical. He dealt with domestic problems, negotiated with China, and fielded military confrontations with foes from the northern border and along the coast. He became a powerful ruler with a strong central government and clear division between its civil and military functions. One of his first acts was to reverse his brother's move and reestablish Hanyang as the capital. Then he went on to further secure his throne.

On closer look, a great amount of the stabilization, beneficial in the abstract, became ruthless on a personal level, leading one to wonder if his adherence to Confucian tenets depended upon their usefulness to his own political advancement. He did whatever he deemed necessary to secure his own family, and through it, the throne. He ordered those relatives killed who might challenge his position and is said to have repositioned his family's early lineage records to fit the new paradigm.

Several factors that came to the fore during King Taejong's rule clearly affected Queen Sindeok: the conformance to Confucian ritual, the importance of the primary wife, and the position of the eldest son. Another item rarely spoken of, but almost daily mentioned in the record, is the fearful and motivating power of portents.

Royal Succession: Unwanted Relatives

Some say that the coup of 1398 came out of Bangwon's personal hatred toward Queen Sindeok, yet she was only one among many. After the palace coup, he continued to eliminate officials, trusted statesmen, in-laws of his own, and in-laws of his son—anyone whom he saw as a threat to the throne. To this end he ruthlessly purged the brothers and their children of his own wife (Yeoheung Min lineage), and after he abdicated and put his son King Sejong on the throne, he ordered King Sejong's wife's father (Sim On) and uncle to kill themselves by drinking poison, thus making it impossible for any in-law-based succession struggle to arise when King Sejong died.[6] Seen in this light, it becomes clear that the actions against Queen Sindeok and her two sons were part of a much larger and farther-reaching royal housecleaning. They simply got in his way.

Revising His Own Lineage

Centuries of Goryeo-style equality prompted most women, and many men, to resist being dragged into the male-dominated Neo-Confucian mode, but it began here in the early 1400s. The country's first comprehensive law code, the *Gyeonggukdaejeon* of 1471, introduced inequality within a family by raising the firstborn son above his brothers and holding him up as the preferred heir.[7] Although for King Taejong it was not yet a law, the importance of the eldest son had been used to his advantage in the coup and in setting up his elder brother as the second king.

Thinking through these principles caused King Taejong to admit that he had no claim to the throne under conditions that he himself had helped set up. His own grandfather had had three wives and his father, Seonggye (King Taejo), was the son of that grandfather's second wife, making King Taejong and all his descendants illegitimate under the new rules. To fix this, King Taejong again took things into his own hands and simply altered the family records. He shifted his grandmother up to become his grandfather's first wife, thereby giving both his father and himself full legitimacy on the throne.

All this shifting shoved his grandfather's first and third wives down into secondary positions and deprived their descendants of any claim to the throne. To erase all doubt, court historians degraded these two women further, to the status of slaves, and ordered their families to return to the northeast area from which they had come. Ironically, at some later (unknown) date the same or subsequent officials returned the record to its original form, giving the birth order accepted today.[8]

The Revolt of 1402

Queen Sindeok's name refused to stay forgotten. Just two years into King Taejong's reign, a rebellion erupted in her name. Governor Jo Saui of Anbyeon and Kang Hyeon (a cousin of Queen Sindeok) launched a violent and well-organized revolt against the state, claiming they were relatives of the queen seeking vengeance for the murder of her two sons. Their rebellion began in the eleventh month of 1402 in Anbyeon and Hamju (modern-day Hamheung) on the east coast and spread west with major battles at Maengsan, Deokcheon, and Anju. The government, however, rallied to crush them without mercy. Within two months, those captured were tortured in the army prosecutor's prison, and two weeks later Jo Saui, Kang Hyeon, and sixteen others were beheaded—the punishment for treason.[9]

Perhaps now Queen Sindeok and her family would fade from the records of the royal court.

Chapter 6

FOUR SIGNIFICANT SITES

The sites in Hanyang that were meant to convey honor to Queen Sindeok—the Jongmyo Shrine (royal ancestral shrine), her royal tomb, and her Buddhist temple—these plus the free-floating tombstones now figure prominently in her prolonged and repeated dishonor. The downfall of this queen is recorded in eleven separate incidents, with the downward spiral spread across twelve years from 1398 to 1410, all of which happened during the reign of King Taejong. It is not clear whether he planned them or simply seized opportunities as they arose, but one by one he erased each remaining trace of this queen.

The first and second dishonors happened so quietly, and were separated by so many years, that they could easily have gone unnoticed, yet they were by far the most significant. The first happened in 1398, when King Jeongjong *1. moved his mother's spirit tablet into a palace hall and moved Queen Sindeok's out.* This simple action foreshadowed the second, for by that substitution he gave Queen Sindeok the single and most overwhelming dishonor—*2. he kept her out of Jongmyo Shrine.* Yet multiple abuses of her tomb, temple, and tombstones accumulated and exacerbated the later controversies.

Jongmyo Shrine

The Jongmyo Shrine is simple and austere, with a calm beauty appropriate for its purpose of honoring the dead. A steep tiled roof and round red pillars run the entire length of the open corridor, and a wide gray stone terrace adds tranquility to the approach. Memorial rites in elaborate Confucian tradition were held, then, to honor the souls of deceased rulers. Now, the same rites indulge the curiosity of tourists.

Two years after King Taejo's death in 1408, the spirit tablets of both the king and Queen Sinui (Lady Han) were enshrined together, publicly proclaiming Queen Sinui as the sole wife of the king. Since by definition, not even a king could have two primary wives, Queen Sindeok's spirit tablet, shifted to her tomb back in 1398, was expected to be forgotten. By virtue of this substitution of spirit tablets, the royal ancestral shrine became the first significant site in her dishonor.[1]

Jeongneung Royal Tomb

Dishonors three through nine took place at the tomb, affording a look at the gradual degradation of the site while it remained in the city and later after being moved to the hills northeast of the city wall. King Taejong could not orchestrate major changes while his father lived, yet changes did occur. As soon as King Jeongjong took the throne in 1398, and without actually touching and defiling Queen Sindeok's tomb, change began.

3. Reducing the number of guards. King Taejong brought about this third dishonor. He reduced the number of guards around the tomb by one hundred (there is no indication of how many guards were there originally) and sent them home.[2]

4. *Building houses on the land.* Because the tomb sat in the center of the capital city where all could see it, many high officials, including Second State Councillor Ha Ryun, wanted it out of the way—they wanted to build their own houses in that prime location. King Taejong agreed. In 1400 he reduced the size of the parklike setting that surrounded the tomb, allowing homes to be built on the land, and then allowing them to crowd ever closer, to within a hundred footsteps of this royal monument.[3]

Major Changes Follow the Death of King Taejo

The death of the retired King Taejo in 1408 cleared the way for major changes. Within a year, King Taejong began systematically deconstructing the tomb site that his father had so meticulously built for his queen.

5. *Moving the tomb.* King Taejong asked the State Council (Uijeongbu) to decide whether Queen Sindeok's tomb should be moved outside the city wall. The officials quoted precedent, saying, "All the royal tombs (near Gaeseong) are outside the city walls yet Jeongneung Royal Tomb is here inside Hanyang. That is not proper. Also, the tomb is very close to the Chinese emissary's lodgings." (Because, of course, King Taejong had allowed the officials to build their homes on that land.) Predictably, the officials recommended the tomb be moved.[4] King Taejong then issued a statement written by Byeon Gyeryang making clear his reasons for the move: (1) In all of history no tomb had been within the gates of the capital, and (2) The tomb was too close to the buildings that housed the Chinese emissary. Good reasons, but one notes that he didn't do it until after

his father's death.[5]

6. *The tombstones.* Thus the tomb was moved—or at least part of it was moved—to a new setting in the hills northeast of the city. The twelve massive spirit-general stones that had surrounded the base of the mound—those elegant stones carved by master carvers and overseen by the governor of Jejudo Island—were left behind on a dump heap. Whether by king's command, simple neglect, or being too large and cumbersome to move, the stones did not follow their tomb. Only the smaller stones and the Goryeo-style stone lantern and table for Confucian ancestor rituals traveled to the new location.[6]

7. *Demolition of the original site.*[*] King Taejong's actions made it clear that Sindeok held no further interest to the court. He ordered the tomb site cleared and allowed all leftover materials used for other purposes. Workers took the timber and stone from the ritual hall (*jeongjagak*) to repair and enlarge the Taepyeonggwan, the house of the Chinese emissary. Finally, orders arrived to completely destroy the site, leaving no trace behind, and for this the workers chiseled away at the stone statues to deface them before leaving them in the dump site.[7]

8. *Attempt to discontinue rituals.* A year and a half later, three days before Queen Sindeok's elaborate death anniversary rituals were scheduled to take place on the tenth day of the eighth month of 1410, the king ordered all ceremonies and rituals canceled. He gave as his reason that she had not been a bona fide wife. The protocol officer cautiously disagreed, reminding the king that Queen Sindeok

---

[*] The original site of the Jeongneung Royal Tomb is memorialized by the street name of Jeong-dong, which runs along next to the small Deoksugung Palace, southwest of Gyeongbokgung Palace, and the site is also the location of the United States ambassador's residence—continuing the precedent of allowing officials to build their homes encroaching upon the tomb's land.

had been the founding king's favorite queen and it would not be appropriate to stop all rituals. The king withdrew his order.[8]

9. Lowering the rank of the tomb. Unable to eliminate the graveside rituals, King Taejong waited two more years and then, on the twenty-third day of the eighth month of 1412, ordered the entire site lowered from rank one (*neung*, the tomb of a king or queen), to rank three (*myo*, the tomb of a prince, princess, or concubine of the king).[9] This new order stripped Queen Sindeok of her royal status and demoted her from wife to concubine. Now that Sindeok had no royal rank, the government need not be responsible for expensive rituals. King Taejong was free to eliminate the morning and evening rituals, plus those of the first and fifteenth days of the month, leaving only the spring and autumn rituals.[10]

With this, the tomb became the second significant site of Queen Sindeok's dishonor.

Queen Sindeok's tomb (top)
Crown Prince Sado and Princess Hyegyeong's tomb (bottom)

Unlike the royal tomb of Crown Prince Sado and Princess Hyegyeong, there are no hedge stones surrounding the mound of Queen Sindeok's tomb.

Heungcheonsa Temple

Heungcheonsa Temple (Rise to Heaven Temple) had been built with King Taejo's personal care and planning, and he had placed it next to Queen Sindeok's tomb specifically for the monks to offer prayers for her spirit. With the tomb moved outside the city in 1409, the temple's original function disappeared, yet it remained in place and continued as the national headquarters for one of the Korean Buddhist sects. During these years, King Taejong expanded his effort to suppress Buddhism and reduce the number of temples across the country, but in honor of his father's dying wish to protect Heungcheonsa Temple, he left it untouched.

10. Replacing her temple with a smaller hermitage. Out of respect for his father's Buddhist faith, King Taejong knew he should not leave Queen Sindeok's tomb without prayers, so when the tomb was moved in 1409, the officials found a small, isolated temple on a hill near the new tomb site and called it Sinheungam Hermitage. The monks there took on the commission to pray for Queen Sindeok's spirit, but soon even this small hermitage was considered too close to the newly relocated tomb.

Before long, they ordered the hermitage moved and sequestered behind a series of steep, forested hills, making Heungcheonsa Temple the third significant site of Queen Sindeok's dishonor.

Tombstones without a Tomb

Flowing from west to east across the royal city, and only slightly south of the palace, runs Cheonggyecheon Stream. Many smaller streams from surrounding mountains feed into this stream and the water then heads east to join the Hangang River. In 1400, only wooden bridges provided crossings.

A violent storm in 1409 set in motion the fourth site of the queen's dishonor, the tombstones themselves. Water raged down the streams, demolishing bridges and eating into the muddy banks. When the rain subsided, the state council recommended that the main bridge over Cheonggyecheon Stream be rebuilt of stone, but to move from wood to the heavy weight of stone meant that the mud-soaked banks of the stream needed major support.

11. From tombstones to bridge supports. Someone suggested that the dump heap be searched for the hedge stones from Queen Sindeok's original tomb and that they be used for this project. King Taejong gave permission and, with tombstones rammed into place along the banks for support, Gwangtonggyo Bridge became the first stone bridge within the city walls.

Why they chose the royal tombstones to support this bridge will never be known. Some blame the workers and others blame King Taejong, but the fact is that they were used and apparently nobody cared, objected, or even noticed the unusual carvings decorating the stones. Workers simply salvaged the stones and shoved them into the mud. One stone sank in upside down, pushing the spirit-general's head beneath the water—and again, whether done carelessly or on purpose, it added to the list of insults heaped upon the queen and her memory.

While the unseen spirit of Queen Sindeok may have been angered by the misuse of the stones, in the visible world the people gradually forgot or never knew that royal stones supported the bridge beneath their feet. And thus the bridge, and the tombstones that supported it, became Queen Sindeok's fourth site of dishonor.

Looking back over these actions (or inactions), it is difficult to see them being fueled by any conscious Confucian thought. King Taejong's honor of his own mother, Queen Sinui, may have been for the sake of her position as first wife, or his wish for proper rites and ceremonies, and his need to follow precedents may have moved Queen Sindeok's tomb out of the city. However, the end result is that King Taejong brought his own mother to the fore and let Queen Sindeok slide out of sight.

As the stones from the Jeongneung Royal Tomb were used as material to build the Gwangtonggyo Bridge, some of them were placed upside down. For example, a stone carved with the Spirit General with his hands clasped in prayer and riding on heavenly clouds stands upside down with his head in the river.

Chapter 7

REPAIRING AND APPEASING

Queen Sindeok, along with her tomb and temple, had been shoved out of sight, but she did not stay away for long. Over the next sixty years Kings Taejong, Sejong, and Sejo each found reason to act in defense of the queen or her two sons.

King Taejong (r. 1400–1418)

Twice in King Taejong's eighteen-year reign, he acted to make amends to some of those dead or alive he had injured in the past. He first moved ahead with restitution for his two half-brothers whom he had murdered just eight years earlier, and ten years later he turned his energies to the survivors of families punished, exiled, or executed at specific times in the past.

Posthumous Names for the Two Murdered Princes: 1406

Each of the two princes whose lives had been taken in the coup of 1398 had been buried in the chaotic aftermath of the trauma without receiving posthumous temple names (*siho*), the official names to be used for their Confucian memorial rites. Now, eight years after their deaths and six years into his reign, on the third day of the eighth month of 1406, King Taejong suddenly ordered a ceremony for each young man, giving Bangbeon the posthumous temple name of Prince Gongsun and Bangseok the posthumous name Prince Sodo.[1]

King Taejong had spent so much energy eliminating male opposition that one wonders what drove him to retrace his steps and honor the memory of these young men. Why had he given temple names to use in rituals when both princes had died without sons, leaving no one to perform such rituals? Perhaps King Taejong's passion for proper rites had caused him to look back and realize that the temple names were missing and without them, rituals could never be performed. He may have felt free to bestow the names now that the princes posed no threat. And there was the ever-present dread of portents and the lurking of restless spirits. His cry of "Only I am to blame [for the unrelenting appearance of portents]" may reveal self-criticism for his earlier cruelties.[2] Unrecorded but equally possible might be a strong urging from his father, the retired King Taejo, still alive at this point and undoubtedly concerned about the restless spirits of his youngest sons unable to settle properly into their graves.

The Great Remorse: 1416, sixth month, twentieth day

Ten years later, in 1416 at age fifty, King Taejong made another powerful reversal that points again to the power of portents. A great drought hit the land. A hundred monks prayed for rain and built ten nine-headed straw dragons to aid their prayer, but still the drought continued.[3] Tormented by his earlier actions, the king sank into a mood of deep remorse, until he became consumed with the need to make things right. He became pensive.

"I have thought long and hard about the cause of the drought (seen as the portent), and it is nowhere else but the incidents of 1398 (palace coup), 1400 (the Second Strife of Princes), and 1402 (executing those in the revolt). I have violated the proper relationship between father and son, and between brothers. However, these were mandated by heaven, and I did not do them with pleasure."[4]

The next day he sat before his officials weeping so loudly he could barely speak. Tears flowed down into his beard. "Because of my lack of virtue, heaven's annoyance has brought about this calamitous drought. I have been in agony day and night. I cannot sleep. No one can imagine what I am going through. Did I become king just so I could wear beautiful clothes? Enjoy good food? Ancient records say that because of the affection heaven has for the ruler, disasters are sent as a warning. How can I ignore these warnings? I must reflect and reform my affairs of state."

Then, asking—indeed, begging—for advice, he encouraged the officials to speak up. "Don't tell me I don't listen to you. I do listen. Even if you say something drastic such as 'Please cut off your hair,' I'll go along with you. Find something [that I can do to reverse this disaster]!"[5]

The officials went to work. They drew up a list of twenty-four actions the king might take to vanquish the drought. Reading the list, King Taejong turned away from it and focused on those three blameworthy events in his own past. He announced royal pardons for all the survivors of the 1398, 1400, and 1402 atrocities and returned to them the right to seek government posts.

The Stepmother Question:
1416, eighth month, twenty-first day

The step-mother question arose once again in 1416, and this time it came with both legal and ritual ramifications. Now a technical issue about precise relationships, it demanded the king's attention and brought forth the twelfth dishonor to Queen Sindeok—not a new one, but indeed a comfortable affirmation of an older one (the ninth dishonor). King Taejong asked official Yu Jeonghyeon for a precise definition of a stepmother (*gyemo*), because suddenly this question needed an answer based not on emotion, but on the complexity of precise mourning rites. He knew that ritual obligations toward a father's second wife (stepmother) dictated that this wife be treated as generously as the first wife, and therefore mourned like the real mother.[6] He also knew that he would be left with a restless spirit, a possible vengeful ghost, if Queen Sindeok's spirit were not properly mourned. What he did not know was the exact definition of "stepmother."

Thus the king found that the new laws put him in an untenable position, and he called for help. If Jeongneung Royal Tomb—note that he did not name Lady Kang, but used her tomb's name instead—had been his stepmother, it was imperative that he reinstate her tomb rituals to the level of his own mother's. But Yu Jeonghyeon replied that a stepmother was one who succeeded a mother who had died. Since Queen Sinui (using Lady Han's honorary title) had still been alive when King Taejong's father married Lady Kang, she could not have been his stepmother. The king responded with relief.

The twelfth dishonor. With the above information, King Taejong confirmed that he had no obligation to Queen Sindeok and he need not reinstate her rituals. "I grew up in my own mother's house, married, and lived separately from Lady Kang. My obligation to Queen Sindeok is only because my father cherished her."[7]

Abdication: 1418

Life hung heavy on King Taejong. In 1417 he cried out in frustration, saying, "If children are not good they cannot take your place. My first two sons are useless and the third is not yet ready. Abdication is impossible, suicide is impossible, so my heart just aches! I cannot die. I cannot escape fate. It pains me."[8]

A year later King Taejong announced his abdication, and this time he meant it. Again he blamed portents, saying that the frost was abnormal and he was the cause. "Long ago we blamed the state councillor, saying the weird portents were his fault. But he died and six others came and went, and all that time the disasters kept coming. Only I have been here all eighteen years, so it must be my own fault."[9]

The king abdicated his throne on the twenty-sixth day of the ninth month of 1418, giving as his reasons his infirmity and the frequent natural disasters. He died four years later. If he thought of Queen Sindeok at all in these final years, it is not recorded.

King Sejong (r. 1418–1450)

King Sejong, the third son of King Taejong, did, however, think of Queen Sindeok. Her name surfaced four times during his reign and each time several forces were at work—his acceptance of ritual, his respect for the past, and his independent thinking.

King Sejong ascended the throne in 1418 and Korea acquired its greatest monarch. Intelligent, creative, and compassionate, he was a man whose erudition held the court spellbound.[10] A partial list of his accomplishments includes the Korean phonetic alphabet hangeul, improved printing techniques, and advances in art, ceramics, technology, agriculture, medicine, and law. Yet above all, much of his work reflects his Neo-Confucian values and his endeavors to implement his Confucian vision of the world.

Two vignettes reveal his personality. As a child, his father thought he spent too much time reading and sent an attendant to take away all his books. King Sejong searched and found one that had escaped notice. With only one book to read, he made do and simply memorized it from beginning to end.[11] Years later, as king, his love of learning continued and when news came to him in the middle of the night that an official had fallen asleep at his desk while studying, the king gave his own robe to a servant with the order to take it and cover the sleeper, so that when he awoke he would know that the king himself valued such devotion to learning.

Following his father's example, King Sejong gradually guided Korea's ceremonial life to conform to the guidelines given in *The House Rules of Master Zhu* (*Zhuzi jiali*), but his actions show he was not bound by the past—he trusted his own mind. He argued with his advisors and occasionally rejected their advice, saying he would not be a slave to the past, that circumstances were different between ancient times and the present.[12]

Aid to the Kang Family: 1418

King Sejong turned his compassion and independent thinking to Queen Sindeok in the very first year of his reign. He knew, of course, that Queen Sindeok had been reduced to a third-rank personage and that all royal caretakers had been removed from her tomb. Thinking it wrong to completely abandon a once-royal tomb, and knowing that even minimal upkeep of the grounds plus rituals (with their various foods, wine, plates, bowls, goblets, and incense) would lay an exorbitant burden on the queen's family, King Sejong asked his officials for advice. The Board of Rites (Yejo) sent a message back to the king reminding him that the state could not perform the ceremonies at a tomb from which honors had been withdrawn, but that the king might help the Kang family with a "rice field tax" amounting to five *gyeol* so that the clan could more easily perform the ceremonies.

Whether the Kangs were given land or money is not clear. The original in Chinese says "rice paddy five units" (*jeon o gyeol*), but the accompanying translation into Korean says "rice paddy tax five units (*jeonse o gyeol*).[13] According to Yi Hong-jik's *Guksadaesajeon*, *gyeol* had several simultaneous meanings. It could mean a parcel of land where one *gyeol* was thirty-three steps in one direction, or the produce from that land, where one *gyeol* is about two bushels, or even a unit of money equivalent to a tax levied and substituted for the actual farm produce.[14]

Whatever the details, King Sejong did reach out to help the Kang family, for it is recorded that "the king so decreed."

Burning Queen Sindeok's Spirit Portrait Scrolls:
1432, first month, eighteenth day

Fourteen years passed before King Sejong again thought of, and apparently turned against, Queen Sindeok, which if true would constitute yet another dishonor. The king ordered the burning of her spirit–portrait scroll (*yeongjeong*), which had been safely housed in

Inanjeon Hall before being moved back to her tomb in 1398. But here again, what seems personal is not. Instead, ancient precedent had won again.

The order from the throne required the burning of *all* portrait scrolls, not only Sindeok's. Upon royal order the Office for the Establishment of Ceremonies (*Uiryesangjeongso*) had ascertained that wooden spirit-tablets, not portraits, conformed to ancient precedent.[15] Chief State Councillor Hwang Hui, from his position next to the throne, put forth the specific reason to avoid spirit portraits. Quoting from Chinese sources, Hwang reported, "Ancient documents (*Geunsarok*, *Mungonggarye*, and *Samagongseoui*) say that when portraits are copied, the hair and beard may not be exactly the same, and thus you will be performing rituals for a different person."

In the past, ritual ceremonies had used both portraits and tablets, with the portraits placed behind the tablets, but Hwang offered another and stronger reason to avoid portraits. Males, he said, could easily have their portraits painted, but no one could draw a portrait of a woman. The new Confucian dynasty ruled that all women had to be sequestered in the inner rooms of their houses, and if they did go out, were required to hide their faces. No portrait painter would get even a glimpse of a woman. Pondering this information, King Sejong decided to use only spirit tablets, and ordered portraits—all of them—burned.[16]

In spite of the edict however, use of spirit portraits did not disappear. Many Joseon kings and scholars tried to conform and use wooden tablets instead of portraits for the rituals, but the traditional custom of using images persisted. King Sejong is an early example of this awkward transition. According to art historian Insoo Cho, King Sejong changed his mind about ancestor portraits more than once.

First he insisted on enshrining the portrait of King Taejong, but around 1431 he shifted to the Confucian idea of rejecting portraits and in 1432 he ordered them burned. Later, he reinstated the use of portraits.[17]

Once Again, a Neglected Tomb: 1434

Hwang Hui gives us the next, almost accidental, account of Queen Sindeok's tomb. Court officials debated the proper care of the tomb for another royal woman. The king asked whether this person had been a concubine or a legitimate queen, and Hwang Hui answered that she had indeed been a legitimate queen. For emphasis, he added, "We should not neglect her, otherwise her tomb will be neglected just like Jeongneung Royal Tomb!"

This small comment tells us that, even though Jeongneung Royal Tomb had been moved out of government control (and sight), Hwang Hui knew and cared about its plight. He didn't want the same neglect to fall on another royal tomb. It also tells us that sometime between 1418 and 1434, for reasons unknown, Queen Sindeok's own family deserted the care of her grave.[18]

Ritual Heirs Provided for the Fallen Princes: 1437

Time had passed—a long time—since King Sejong's father had given the murdered princes their temple names in 1406. Now, thirty-one years later, King Sejong noticed that although the boys had proper names, they had no descendants to carry out ancestor rituals for them. Pondering this, he devised a plan to bring the princes' ceremonies into line with Confucian teaching, and discussed with his advisors the requirements of a proper heir to perform such duties.

The three state councillors, with Hwang Hui still the chief, spoke in front of the king.

"In the olden days," he said, "if a family had no one to perform ancestor rituals, they adopted the son of a relative to be the legitimate heir, just to perform the rituals. There is no argument on this point. However, when you look at ancient writings from China, the book of protocol raises the question of who is the legitimate heir. It must be [a person from] the same clan, a blood relative. Heaven does not accept rituals done by the wrong person. On the other hand, if there is no son, then the family can appoint the son of a relative and thereafter he will be considered the real son of those parents. But be careful! He cannot go back and do rites for his own birth parents."[19]

Being assured that an adoptee from the same clan—the son of a relative—would be considered the real son of his adoptive parents, King Sejong made his decision, saying, "The two murdered princes died without descendants and thus have no legitimate heirs. Therefore, I appoint my fifth son, Grand Prince Gwangpyeong (1425-1444) to be [the] son of the widow of Bangbeon, and my sixth son, Grand Prince Geumseong (1426-1457), to be the son of [the] widow of Bangseok. As sons, they will establish memorials and perform ancestor rituals in honor of the two princes."[20]

Five months later, on the twenty-seventh day of the eleventh month of 1437, the king established memorials, performed ceremonies, and gave posthumous titles to both princes, restoring full honors to their memorial tablets.

But nothing remains stable for long.

King Sejo (r. 1455–1468)

Here is yet another surprise, for just as it seemed that everything was settled with regard to the memory of Queen Sindeok and her sons, another monarch took up the cause. King Sejo enters the story.

King Sejo, although a son of King Sejong, was not the dynasty's fifth king, but its seventh. Two other kings, an elder brother and a nephew, had each had a very short reign and King Sejo's attempt to secure the throne for himself had produced a bloody succession struggle similar to those that had rocked the dynasty in the past. However, once he had eliminated his opposition, this king followed somewhat in the footsteps of his father, King Sejong. Well educated and devoted to his studies, he moved on to become another of Korea's most able monarchs. He stabilized the country, strengthened the monarchy, improved the national economy, and along the way made a sustained effort to benefit the common people. And in the very first years of his reign, he encountered Queen Sindeok and her family.

When King Sejo acted in behalf of the dynasty's founding family, it raised again the relentless question of why. Why would this man be moved to act in Queen Sindeok's behalf? Why would he even think of her? Did he act as king, consulting earlier precedent, observing Confucian rituals, placating unseen spirits—or was it the man, looking back with remorse over the treatment given to his great-grandfather's family? Perhaps, unable to undo the actions of past monarchs, he chose to do something on his own. Whatever the reasons, King Sejo began his reign with two actions honoring the dynasty's founding family.

Restoring a Broken Ritual Line

While King Sejo was actively eliminating opposition to his own rule, he had executed many of those who had plotted against him, including his brother Grand Prince Geumseong. This young man was the prince King Sejong had appointed in 1437 to perform the ancestor rituals for the murdered Grand Prince Uian (Bangseok). Now Grand Prince Geumseong too was dead and the line of ritual descendants was again broken. Almost immediately, however, King Sejo realized the break (or an official pointed it out to him) and he chose to honor the precedent set in place by his father. Having eliminated one ritual heir, he appointed another of his father's grandsons to take Grand Prince Geumseong's place, thus continuing the line of heirs for Queen Sindeok's fallen prince.[21]

The Great Bronze Bell: 1461

A great bronze bell hangs unnoticed in the courtyard of the small Deoksugung Palace in Seoul. Every temple has a bell, and this one seems no different than all the others until one reads the information board in front of the bell's pavilion. It announces that Grand Prince Hyoryeong, the second son of King Taejong (also a sixty-five-year-old uncle of King Sejo), had ordered it cast in 1461 specifically to pray for the repose of Queen Sindeok's soul.

A bell for Queen Sindeok? Why a bell, and why then? Consider. Just four years earlier King Sejo had arranged to continue the ritual line for the murdered prince, and now King Sejo's uncle was ordering that a great bronze bell be cast. The two acts must be connected. One can only think that, as King Sejo repaired the ritual line for the prince, his elderly uncle learned of it and began thinking of the

Bronze Bell with Inscription of
"Heungcheonsa Temple"

prince's mother, the queen who had died the very year he (Grand Prince Hyoryeong) was born.

A great bronze bell is no trinket. It is huge, heavy, and expensive. Why then, and why by this elderly uncle so far removed from the original action? He knew that construction of Heungcheonsa Temple had been planned and overseen by his grandfather and it had been consecrated to Lady Kang, and perhaps he knew, as his father King Taejong had known, that King Taejo had cherished his young wife.[22] Now the grounds were overrun by the bustling business of the National Buddhist Center, and nothing remained to suggest the temple's intended use. Thus the bell was cast and hung on the original site to renew, in part, the purpose for which King Taejo had built the temple—that prayers might rise again from the grounds of his queen's original place of honor.

The bell stayed in place until 1510, when Heungcheonsa Temple burned to the ground. The great bell then began to meander around Seoul. It moved to the Dongdaemun Gate (Great East Gate) and then to the belfry of Gwanghwamun Gate, the gate to Gyeongbokgung Palace. During the Japanese colonial period (1910–1945) it hung in Changgyeonggung Palace, and finally it was moved to its current home in Deoksugung Palace, perhaps because this small palace sits on land close to the original grounds of Heungcheonsa Temple.

The great bronze bell, placed by royal decree and commemorating both the queen and her temple, stands as a solid monument to close out this part of Queen Sindeok's story.

And then came the silence.

Part Three

IDEOLOGICAL WARFARE

(1500–1669)

內蘊之精采得之

長八小塘之神籲

妙運不專在

於眉目毛髮

微底月滿

邃頂疏貴

題為

安君五十

真影

燈影庵

主

Portrait of Scholar-official Ahn in his Fifties Year, 19th century, Yi Chaegwan
(1783-1387), hanging scroll, ink and color on silk, LACMA collections

Chapter 8

THE RISE OF
THE SCHOLAR-OFFICIALS

After a silence of 120 years Queen Sindeok's name again came before the court, but this time it was not the kings who dominated the action, but court officials. Year after year these men came before the throne both individually and in ever-increasing numbers as they asked, argued, and pleaded that past wrongs be made right. Each monarch in turn simply held his ground and refused to change that which he deeply believed could not be changed.

The Controversy

Stripped of all permutations, the question so vehemently argued by the court scholars dealt with only one thing: Was she, or was she not, a legitimate wife and thus a legitimate queen? And if she was legitimate, it was imperative that she be restored to all attendant honors—a restoration that required two clear actions: (1) the restoration of her derelict tomb and (2) the entering of her spirit tablet into the royal ancestral shrine, Jongmyo Shrine.

The problem from the monarch's perspective focused on the same unanswerable question—whether Queen Sindeok was a legitimate queen or not—and since the answer was elusive at best, they dared not move on her behalf. In the case of the tomb, offering maintenance still hinged on whether or not Queen Sindeok's burial place was a royal tomb deserving of state care (landscaping, memorial hall, posting a caretaker and guards) or a simple grave and of no import to the government. Not having an answer, kings gave the matter little attention.

Enshrinement at Jongmyo Shrine, on the other hand, demanded a decision that no king dare tackle. Was she royalty or not? An answer to this would eliminate the need for the other checks and balances, but no one had the answer. No matter how deeply scholars searched, opposing information continued to surface. Faced with this overwhelming and unanswerable question, kings simply refused to take action. To enter a spirit tablet in the royal ancestral hall established that person as a legitimate, indisputable member of Joseon royalty, and that the kings feared to do. They were terrified of placing her, perhaps in error, in this sacrosanct shrine, which by its very name was reserved for royalty.

Intangible Constraints

One might reasonably ask why one of the monarchs didn't simply make a decision, rule one way or the other, and end the controversy. And the answer, of course, is that nothing is simple. Layers of constraint lay heavy on the throne: the mandate of heaven, filial piety, and an overpowering need to follow a precedent—which in Queen Sindeok's case did not exist.

The mandate of heaven. The heavenly mandate—an intangible expectation—implied that if a king ruled wisely, heaven gave him the mandate to continue and blessings followed. Each king in turn believed he ruled under this mandate. Thus any departure from what an earlier ruler had done implied that the previous ruling had been a mistake. Each monarch thus refused to act in Queen Sindeok's behalf out of loyalty to the omniscience of his royal predecessors, reasoning that a ruler acting under the mandate of heaven could not have been in error.

Filial piety. In like manner, to act against a decision of a royal ancestor, each one a descendant of Yi Seonggye, also implied that the early decision had been a mistake, and for a filial son to tell a father—an ancestor—he was wrong was not an option.

Need for a precedent. Mencius states it clearly: "No one ever erred [by] following the example of the [former king]."[1] From the sage-kings of mythical China down to the Joseon monarchs, all the statesmen, philosophers, and historical figures were held up as examples by which the sovereign should rule. The bureaucrats resorted to history with impunity in their contests for power with the king, but by the same token, the king could do the same.[2] Ancient precedent was studied whenever a new social policy had to be devised. When it was not possible to find such suitable evidence, the making of decisions came to a halt and at times was delayed for years, as is clearly seen in the case of Queen Sindeok.

Tangible Constraints

The Three Boards. During the discussions before the throne, officers of the Three Boards (Samsa) are much in evidence, for they existed specifically to review and censure the work of the government. The Office of Remonstrance/Censor-General (Saganwon) had some fifty men who could criticize the king directly; the Office of the Inspector-General (Saheonbu) with some thirty men, criticized other government bodies and often branched out (unofficially) to join others in criticism of the king; the Office of Special Counselors (Hongmungwan) dealt with historical precedents, drafted documents, and advised and admonished the king.[3] Through these three offices, the bureaucrats attempted to control each other and hold the king to the right path (as they perceived it), often to the extreme frustration of the monarch.

Orthodox Confucianism. During the middle of the Joseon period, Confucian scholars grew increasingly orthodox and increased their efforts to extend Confucian procedures into all decisions, so that large or small, each must be advanced, argued, and justified by Confucian rhetoric. In every situation, Queen Sindeok's included, scholars and monarchs argued their positions with zeal, absolutely convinced that the fundamental principles of Neo-Confucianism were valid at all times and in all places, and that any belief or tradition that did not comply must be rejected as heretical. These men deliberated everything—state affairs, missions to foreign lands, the writing of missives, and the production of literary works. They mounted accusations, defenses, exhortations, and pleas. They prepared scrupulously, citing historical precedents, classical allusions, and other devices all aimed to produce the desired verbal effect.[4] The arguments of these Confucian ritualists were overpowering. No one could have denied their doctrinal validity.

The main venue for these debates and deliberations, of course, was the royal court, for the Korean king involved himself directly in every detail of government. Yet when reading the seemingly free exchanges between these officials and the throne, it is easy to be misled. Yes, they cajoled and argued, but they were trained to choose their topics and their words carefully, fully aware of the power of the monarch. Every word had to be considered and weighed, as a lack of decorum or the inclusion of a taboo word could unleash the king's anger. In a Confucian state, ideology and the king's authority had to adjust to each other, yet even the powerful scholar-officials knew that the final decision rested with the king.[5]

Power of factions. The reality of factions seizing political control is not new, but the factions that surfaced in Korea during the late 1500s were far more than temporary alliances; they were permanent, polarized groups that grew more powerful as the centuries progressed. These groups developed with two major distinctions: They were led by Neo-Confucian scholars, and they stayed together over generations out of faithfulness to the positions of their founders. The Confucian concepts of filial piety and family loyalty—whether by birth, marriage, or student-teacher affiliations—forced men into factions from which they could not escape.

These political factions continually undermined the rule of mid-Joseon kings with contests whose origins ranged from personal enmity to vague and abstract principles to competition for control of government agencies. The arguments often reached fever pitch, tearing the court apart, as their quest for moral perfection admitted only one correct stance, making opposition not only disloyal but immoral. Confucianism forced every issue to be seen as black or white, with no room for gray and with no mechanism for compromise.

The scholar Song Siyeol. The scholar Song Siyeol (1607–1689), along with his contemporary Song Jungil (1606–1672), played a pivotal role in Queen Sindeok's controversy. These men were two of the strongest and most esteemed of the mid-Joseon factional leaders and both were gifted writers and recognized authorities on ritual and orthodox procedures. The climate of the times supplied a perfect opening for them. According to Deuchler, the 1600s was a time when men took extreme positions about rituals and interpretation of the classics, with the intensity of their views often expressed in fierce criticism of opposition. Their focus was not philosophical but tangible, focusing on clarity of ritual.[6] Song Siyeol had devoted his life to the study of Neo-Confucianism and it was said of him that "whoever does not give Zhu Xi credit as an important scholar cannot understand Confucius, and whoever does not follow Song Siyeol's teaching cannot understand Zhu Xi."[7] Song appointed himself guardian of Zhu Xi's philosophical heritage in Korea. He was tireless, uncompromising, and lashed out fiercely at opponents.

Thus the controversy surrounding Queen Sindeok found no answer. Men quoted commentaries, but the books did not agree. They searched for a precedent but found only conflicting situations and debated which one to emulate. Yet while the debates continued, a surprising number of people did approach the throne specifically to gain redress for this one queen—lesser officials (Yi Chang, Yi Uigeon), a local governor (Choe Myeonggil), and unknowns (Kang Sunil, Kang Cheonik) alike. They came, reminding the king that although Queen Sindeok was officially ignored, outside the court people remembered her. "It is known that the descendants have continued the line" (1581), "I am a seventh-generation descendant" (1582), and "Ever since I was a child I've heard of her" (1669). Each one came with a request, received a hearing, and had to accept the action or lack thereof that his monarch was willing to take.

The arguments continued. The tasks remained undone. Queen Sindeok remained an enigma.

Chapter 9

A YOUNG MAN'S REQUEST

King Seonjo (r. 1567–1608)

For nearly two hundred years there had been no reference to Queen Sindeok at the royal court. Now, on the first day of the eleventh month of 1581, two things happened almost simultaneously: The Three Boards (*samsa*), with no obvious provocation, appealed to the king to restore Queen Sindeok's honor, and a young man approached King Seonjo, invoked the name of Queen Sindeok, and in so doing helped spark the court's renewed interest in the queen's plight. These two incidents together raise the question of why this queen on this day.

Two possibilities suggest themselves, one from the official records of King Seonjo's *Sillok* and one from the unofficial record of Yi Geung-ik. Together, they catapult the court into a three-year odyssey.

Looking Back

When looking for the cause of an action, one generally looks back at what happened "just before," and in this case it appears that the *Sillok* of 1581—the record for the sixteenth day of the tenth month—notes that the court was again deep in apprehension of portents as hail beat down on the crops and lightning strikes ignited fires. King Seonjo commented, as kings had done before him, that it was the monarch's responsibility to alleviate the frightening omens by some restorative action. He sent workers out to inspect the damage and called officials together to offer solutions to stop the continuous hail, thunder, and lightning. Officials attempted to calm the king, saying that they no longer believed such phenomena to be the result of a king's actions. History books, they said, were full of natural disasters during the reigns of good kings.

On the other hand, the renowned scholar Yi I (also known as Yi Yulgok) realized the king's nervousness and suggested that the king might select a qualified person to honor and elevate to a higher position. He suggested the government posthumously honor either the reformer Jo Gwangjo or the philosopher Yi Hwang, although both men had been dead for years. The king accepted the idea but made no decision, asking instead for more practical recommendations. On that day, no one had a suggestion, and the thunder and lightning continued.[1]

And then the *Sillok* becomes silent. For the following two weeks, the crucial weeks in this discussion, there is no entry. Thus one is left to wonder if the portents continued, or if other suggestions were made to set the king's mind at ease. It is possible, following Yi I's suggestion of posthumous honors, that someone suggested Queen Sindeok. But if so, it remains unknown. The original *Sillok* has tenth-month entries for days one, sixteen, and seventeen, and the supplement version has only day one for the entire month. What became of those two weeks?

The mystery of the empty *Sillok* disappears, however, when we look at the larger picture of Korean history. King Seonjo reigned from 1567 to 1608 and about two-thirds into his reign, in 1592, the Japanese army invaded Korea, the king fled, and much of Seoul became engulfed in fighting, looting, and fires—and with that, many of the records that upon the king's eventual death would have been gathered into his *Sillok* instead were lost in the fray. In fact, for the first twenty-five years of his reign, fully half of his material is missing, including those two weeks at the end of the tenth month of 1581.

The story does pick up again at the beginning of the eleventh month, but the gaps continue, with the original *Sillok* containing only days one, four, and seventeen and then jumping to the middle of the twelfth month, and the supplement offering only the first day of the eleventh month and then the first day of the twelfth. Yet even with this paucity of records, we clearly witness the unyielding determination of scholars as they search for arguments strong enough to sway the equally unyielding monarch. And the scribes of the *Sillok*, who generally present events with little emotion, here record the stress mounting on both sides as the debate wore on month after month.

King Seonjo is often remembered as the king who gave way to panic and fled the capital when the Japanese invaded in 1592, but he might instead be respected for his tenacious personality. His profound commitment to Confucian values shows clearly in another incident in his reign, again related to the Japanese invasion of 1592. A Chinese official, Ding Yingtai, presented a document in 1598 saying the Korean king "had deceived the Son of Heaven," the Chinese emperor. This verbal attack stunned the king and set him to pondering some serious questions. If, as Confucius taught, loyalty was an obligation of the king to the emperor, what happened when the king was accused of disloyalty? Disloyalty to one's lord must be treason. If so, could a king be a king and a traitor at the same time? Unable to reconcile his ideal with this accusation, King Seonjo retired to his private apartment, closed the doors, and refused to come out. If he could not live up to his ideal, he was not fit to rule. Court officials, not so idealistic, begged him to return to work, saying the country needed a ruler, even one who was less than perfect. They wore away at the king's stance hour by hour, switching arguments, changing phrases, until finally the king gave in and returned to office.[2]

This is the same king who in 1581 faced the barrage of officials requesting redress for Queen Sindeok, and refused them all with the same hold on his beliefs.

Kang Sunil Speaks Up: 1581, eleventh month

Yi Geung-ik opens the eleventh month by recounting a significant event in this recurrence of Queen Sindeok's name—but without giving the day. If indeed it happened on the morning of the first day of the month, it supplies a clear prompt to the entry of the Three Boards. It began with a young man's request.

King Seonjo regularly went out into the city and could be seen riding his horse about the capital.[3] On this day, appearing unannounced, a certain young man named Kang Sunil used his youthful bravado to approach the king's procession with a specific request—he wanted out of his obligatory military service and he knew how to make it happen. He claimed to be a descendant of Kang Yunseong, Queen Sindeok's father, and said he had come from his home in Deogwon to the capital to make a direct appeal to the king. "I am drafted to serve in the military," he said, "but I implore that I be spared. I know there is a precedent of waiving military duty for a person who would pay homage to a national tomb, and I wish to claim that precedent to attend my ancestor's tomb. Please, Your Majesty, give permission."[4]

Kang Sunil thus brought to the fore a practice that had been put in place by King Taejo at the beginning of the dynasty to care for three generations of the king's own female ancestors, all of whom had tombs in the north. He had assigned one man to tend each tomb, and in exchange he had waived their military duties.

Yi I overheard Kang Sunil's request and stepped forward to advise the king, saying they should not ignore it. Indeed, no justifiable reason explained why Queen Sindeok's memory had been forgotten and her rituals ignored. Such neglect violated the Confucian ethical and moral code; therefore, as the boy suggested, they must care for her tomb and resume ceremonies honoring her.[5]

But where was this tomb? No one had thought of it in over a hundred years and no one seemed to know.

The Three Boards

Now on this very same day, the first day of the eleventh month, the Three Boards (Saheonbu, Saganwon, and Hongmungwan) knelt before the king asking that he restore Queen Sindeok's honor. Needing a precedent, they lifted up another dishonored queen, saying that ever since King Seongjong's reign (1469–1494) there had been scholars who had appealed asking that Soreung Royal Tomb (using the tomb's name to stand for Queen Hyeondeok) be restored. Those scholars had continued to argue until eventually Soreung Royal Tomb was restored, and now it was time to do the same for Jeongneung Royal Tomb (using the tomb name to stand for Queen Sindeok). This stood as the example of what could and should be done for Queen Sindeok, for Soreung Royal Tomb involved a case in many ways similar to Queen Sindeok's own situation. The queen, who had died in 1441, had also been reduced to the status of a commoner and refused entry into the ancestral temple even though she was demonstrably blameless and unflawed. King Jungjong (r. 1506–1544), coming to the throne just sixty-five years after her death, had recognized the injustice and rehabilitated her.

Officials insisted that the only protocol missing in the entire country was the care of Queen Sindeok. They informed the king that the illustrious Ming emperor of China had sent condolences at her death acknowledging Queen Sindeok as the legitimate wife of King Taejo, who had loved her and given her great respect. Despite this, when he died, his sons honored their own mother and abandoned altogether the rituals for Queen Sindeok. Now it was time to right this wrong.

But the king refused, saying too much time had elapsed.[6]

Written Documents

The Three Boards strengthened their position, saying King Taejo had prepared a jade book in which Queen Sindeok was praised. When titles were conferred posthumously upon Confucian royalty along with descriptions of their virtuous lives, these were entered into an inscribed royal record, a jade book (*okchaek*). Queen Sindeok was included there because Taejo himself had entered her name.[7]

The pressure continued as scholars approached the throne, this time with news about the location of Queen Sindeok's tomb. Their archival search had turned up an old document written by Byeon Gyeryang, a scholar who had worked as director of the Office of Royal Decrees during the reign of Kings Taejong and Sejong, and this document (*Chunjeongjip*) told that Queen Sindeok's tomb had been moved to the northeast of Seoul. With this directive, King Seonjo ordered a search party to go off in that direction.[8] But before they left, Yi Chang heard the mention of Kang Sunil's ancestry and came forward announcing that he also was a descendant of Queen Sindeok on his mother's side. "It is known that descendants have continued the line," he said, "yet even we cannot find the tomb." With that, the king ordered him to go with the search party.

They went from mountain to mountain without success. Ridge upon ridge rose up in a jagged disarray like the convolutions of crumpled paper, all alike, all overgrown with trees and vines, berries and acacia thorns, so that even a large royal grave mound could be hidden in the growth. Finally the royal search party came upon a village at the foot of a mountain, and were told that farther up the mountain they could find a very neglected tomb lying in ruins.[9] Yet even then nothing was done.

King Taejo's Heavenly Tears

For the next three days in a row came three reports written by the scholar Chae Jeunggwang. The third report reminded the court that in Goryeo customs both wives had been equal, yet after their deaths only one had been honored. Thus if the court officials now argued that only one could be the legitimate wife (*jeongbae*), they must determine which set of customs they meant to follow, those of Goryeo or those of Joseon.

Chae's report continued, but added the safety net of putting the blame on the workers rather than a former king. He said that when King Taejong became king, a few subjects had stirred up problems by trying to reduce the rank of the queen and denigrate her position by reducing her titles and moving the tomb. Although King Taejong went along with it, it was known that while Queen Sindeok was alive, King Taejong served her with respect and honor. "If we continue to neglect Queen Sindeok," Chae wrote, "then King Taejo in heaven will be shedding tears of frustration that his beloved queen is not honored on earth."[10]

The *Sillok* skips to the twelfth month, and we find that nothing had changed. Two of the boards appealed to the king's conscience and filial duty. "You are an intelligent monarch, so you should know this, Your Majesty. Why do you refuse to fix the tomb? Surely a well-cared-for tomb was the true intention of the earlier king." On the eighteenth day, they brought up King Sejong, saying that he had written memorial tablets for both Queens Sindeok and Sinui, which meant that even King Sejong regarded the two queens as equal and yet they honored one and neglected the other.[11]

The king became annoyed. "I already told you I can never give permission. Why do you continue bothering me?" Nevertheless, they persisted. The titles of the two queens' tombs (Jeongneung for Lady Kang and Jereung for Lady Han) were equal, yet proper respect had been paid to one and not the other. The eulogies had been equal, yet Queen Sindeok's was gone. As time went on, the tomb itself had disappeared and been forgotten, so that now they, the descendants, had the honor of correcting this wrong. "Please, Your Majesty, let us restore the tomb."

Daily searching to refine their arguments, the officials presented a new thought, saying that Lady Kang had actually been the more correct of King Taejo's two spouses and that her status and title were clearly written in King Sejong's ode *Yongbieocheonga* (Song of Dragons Flying to Heaven). Now, she had simply been ignored. Considering the ethics of heaven and earthly righteousness, this could not have been King Taejo's intent.

Still refusing to give up, officials put forth new arguments, until finally the king lost his patience. "Listen to me! You will never accomplish your goal, so why don't you get on with your own jobs!"[12]

Undaunted, the censor-general and the inspector-general asked, "How can we ignore our founding queen? We cannot go back to our own jobs while this unrighteousness continues. Do not delay. One day delayed is one day lost."

The king again said no. The officials became even more intense, now saying that Sindeok's honor must be restored in not one, but two ways: they must refurbish her tomb and they must also install her tablets in Jongmyo Shrine. Exasperated, the king exclaimed, "If it were something I could do, you know I would. But I cannot. This event is long past. If they did not fix this situation long ago, there must have been a reason. I cannot change it now!"[13]

A Seventh-Generation Descendant

Midway into the second year, another descendant appeared before the king. The government official Yi Uigeon claimed to be a seventh-generation descendant of the queen and submitted a list of all the good things Lady Kang had done, how she had helped King Taejo and was the Mother of the Nation. His relative, Yi Chang, summarized the appeal thusly:

> Now times have changed. There is no one watching over her tomb, the tomb is in great disrepair, and it has been like this for the last two hundred years. Who, with hot blood in his veins, would not feel greatly disturbed?
>
> Finally the day has come to correct this wrong. This is the time

to resume giving honors to her. Near the tomb, stones are scattered here and there and wild animals from the nearby woods frequently invade this holy space. Wood gatherers and hunters use the spirit path, which at all the other tombs is protected. Neglect is extreme.

Yet the king and royal officials have not provided for appropriate rituals to be performed. Therefore we, the descendants, request that while awaiting the royal decree, we may proceed with honoring her.[14]

With numbing precision, the Three Boards continued their appeals on into the early months of the third year, 1583, where finally the king shifted his stance and appointed Gi Daejeong to study the correctness of government policy. A week later Gi returned, urging the king to agree with his officials.[15]

In spite of all this pressure, the king remained stubborn. His tenacity was overpowering, and his answers never wavered. Thus after eighteen months of unrelenting struggle, the officials acknowledged the futility of their attempts. They bowed to their king's decision, knowing that he would not—or could not—bend his stance.

The King's Decision

Holding firm, King Seonjo absolutely refused to deal with the Jongmyo Shrine request, and granted only some meager care of the tomb. He ordered a caretaker (*bongsik*) and guard (*suchong*) placed at the tomb and gave permission for the performance of rituals, once a year on Hansik day, 105 days after the winter solstice. Many, it is said, refused to be thankful for the king's token concession, and instead regretted that rituals could be done only once a year, not even on special days such as the anniversary of the queen's birth or of her funeral.[16]

The debate had lasted into its third year. As a result of the ritualists' campaign before the throne, the king did order a search for Queen Sindeok's neglected tomb, but he remained resolutely opposed to any rehabilitation, and he held his ground. The scholars got nothing from him other than repairs and restoration of the tomb and a commitment to hold an annual ritual. He absolutely refused to enter her into the Jongmyo Shrine. One wonders if the young man, Kang Sunil, ever realized that his simple request before the king back in 1581 may have been part of this royal argument that had in the end resulted in only one small concession.

Chapter 10

ONE DECADE, TWO EXTREMES

Thirty years passed quietly after the young Kang Sunil took part in the futile efforts to restore honor to Queen Sindeok, and then within a decade her name arose twice. Two men—one a king, the other a local governor—called forth Queen Sindeok's name within only a few years of each other, each for extremely different purposes, and each with equally different results.

King Gwanghaegun's Insidious Search

King Seonjo's second son, King Gwanghaegun (r. 1608–1623), wished only to learn the details of Queen Sindeok's dishonor for his own sinister reasons. He had no intention of restoring her tomb or her honor.

King Gwanghaegun had skills that should have been used in both domestic and foreign affairs, yet he became one of only two Joseon kings forced off the throne and thus denied a posthumous kingly title such as *jo* or *jong*. His rule began ten years after the end of the devastating Japanese invasions under Hideyoshi that had left Korea with immense damage throughout the country, and King Gwanghaegun took action to deal with the needed reconstruction.

He rebuilt the history archives, reprinted many books destroyed during the war, and renovated the country's woefully inadequate military training program. Modern historians generally see King Gwanghaegun as a good king ruined by the factional splits of his time.[1] During his reign, his contemporaries, however, lined up against him as he tried to remain neutral in the conflict between the Ming and the Jurchen (later called Manchu)—a pragmatic foreign policy intended to keep Korea out of the fighting. Other writers vilified him, saying he lacked loyalty and was coarse, addicted to tobacco (imported from Japan in 1616), and responsible for the death of his little half-brother, who had suffocated in an overheated room.

The Need for Information

It was yet another succession disaster that made this king think of Queen Sindeok. His story will sound familiar. King Gwanghaegun was the son of a royal concubine (*hugung*), and his father, King Seonjo, had no son by his first queen. However, King Seonjo later married a second wife, young Queen Inmok (1584–1632). In 1606 she bore a son, and in 1608 the king died. Thus when King Gwanghaegun ascended the throne at his father's death, he had a two-year-old half-brother born to a woman who, unlike his own mother, was a fully royal legitimate queen. The birth of this young half-brother posed an immediate threat to King Gwanghaegun, for many at court supported the child, saying that since his mother was a legitimate queen, that child should be heir to the throne. Others stood by King Gwanghaegun.

King Gwanghaegun immediately went into action to secure the throne and, one by one, removed all potential rivals, exiling or beheading them for treason. By 1613 his rule had become devastatingly cruel and his ill treatment targeted Queen Inmok and her (by then) seven-year-old son. King Gwanghaegun accused the child of treason and, along with his supporters, exiled him to Ganghwado Island. That left one major problem—what should now be done with this young prince and his mother, Queen Inmok.

Queen Sindeok as a Royal Precedent

King Gwanghaegun thought back to the situation at the beginning of the dynasty and realized that the treatment given Queen Sindeok and her sons might supply him a needed precedent and a pattern for action against his own half-brother and the child's mother. On the twenty-sixth day of the fifth month of 1613, the king ordered officials in the Office of State Archives (Chunchugwan) to search the ancient documents and find everything concerning Queen Sindeok and her two murdered sons. They were to look from King Taejo to King Taejong, investigate the details of the princes' arrest and execution and the circumstances under which Queen Sindeok had been deprived of her royal rank, and report back to him in writing. He needed to know how King Taejong had treated Queen Sindeok in order to make his own plans to abrogate the position and status of Dowager Queen Inmok.[2] The officials did locate some information, but apparently not the details the king needed, for arguments raged on day after day without any decision.

A year later the eight-year-old Grand Prince Yeongchang was brought back to the city and confined to a palace room where soon, suspiciously, he smothered in an overheated room. His mother remained a problem. Three years later the king resumed his crusade against this queen and now the officials urged caution. They pointed out that Queen Inmok's situation differed significantly, as Sindeok's status had not been lowered until after her death, whereas Queen Inmok was very much alive. Perhaps, they said, Sindeok's situation was not a good example to follow.[3] Finally they simply took away the queen's royal status and placed her under house arrest, where she remained for the next five years.

As for the king, officials deposed him in 1623, sent him into exile, and restored Queen Inmok to her position as dowager queen. The need to consider Queen Sindeok sank from sight until the next king received a disturbing report.

King Injo (r. 1623–1649)

Governor Choe Requests Help

Twelve years passed and then Queen Sindeok's name came again before the court. This time the plea was in her favor. Choe Myeonggil, the governor of Gyeonggi-do province, approached the throne in 1629 to make his annual report on the care of the royal tombs. Quite unexpectedly, he focused attention on the tomb of Queen Sindeok and requested help.[4] He reported that he had surveyed all nineteen royal tombs during the annual autumn inspection tour and found each of them in disrepair with weeds growing out of control. Choe continued:

> Every year we pull the weeds where we can reach them, but we do not dare touch the top of each mound without first having a proper ceremony, so gradually the weeds have taken over. In my humble consideration, it is a dilemma. On one hand, we should not touch

the top of the tombs, but on the other hand, it is not proper that the weeds keep growing. I humbly suggest that we supply both guards and workers to various tombs. We especially found Queen Sindeok's tomb, Jeongneung, to be full of weeds. It is the tomb of King Taejo's queen and therefore more important than many others. Despite that, there is just a low-ranking official there, who is not familiar with royal rituals. There is no official administrator (*chambong*) entrusted to perform ceremonies. Also, there used to be a memorial hall but it is in ruins, so to do any ceremony at all, we would have to pitch a tent.[5]

The governor continued:

This neglect had been going on so long that it might not even be appropriate to mention it. But because there was no guard at Jeongneung Royal Tomb, the local woodsmen and cowherds took turns chopping down trees, thus making it a sorry state of affairs. Please, at least put some caretaker there to forbid the tree cutting and truly, we should rebuild the hall. The minister of protocol told me that we must send workers to pull down those weeds, yet I know it is not proper to climb on the tomb mound. In the past we always had a cabinet-level minister perform the ceremony. Now, Jeongneung Royal Tomb has no administrator and no guard. We must send these proper workers.

This report immediately became a dilemma with no solution— doomed by the continuing struggle between the need for proper protocol on one hand and the need for a proper precedent on the other. The king did agree to send workers to the tomb but could not approve ceremonies since there was no ceremonial hall (*jeongjagak*) and he had no precedent for rebuilding it.

Thus again a monarch found himself caught between respecting Queen Sindeok's royal status and fearing to take responsibility for reconstruction. The subject disappeared for another forty years, until a much more heated controversy divided the court and occupied the energies of all the royal personnel.

Chapter 11

CRESCENDO

King Hyeonjong (r. 1659–1674)

The year 1669 began as any other year, but almost immediately it became the most crucial in Queen Sindeok's story. It became the turning point, for the wandering restless spirit of Queen Sindeok found its long-sought advocate in the most eminent of scholars, Song Siyeol. The fight he took on lasted eight months and involved an ever-increasing number of scholars, who presented ever more convincing arguments before the throne, until finally the king did what no king before him had dared to do—he agreed to their demands.

An extraordinary feature of this new fight was that Song gained support even from members of severely hostile factions, although many of them had stated that they no longer felt the need for such rituals. On this one subject of the queen, however, Song drew these men onto common ground as he emphasized that these rituals were a vital and mutually accepted part of their ancestral heritage, yet had so glaringly been withheld from Queen Sindeok. In retrospect, this year of agreement is of utmost importance, for it was the unanimity of the scholars that forced the king to concede, and their agreement is the more remarkable for within another five years the same men battled yet again over another set of royal funeral rites, this time to the threat of exile and even death.[1] The question arises—and begs exploration—as to why this man sustained such an arduous campaign for the enshrinement of this one queen, and why at that particular moment in time.

Song Siyeol was no ordinary scholar. He was a champion of Confucian orthodoxy, called by his friends fierce, passionate, outspoken, and aggressive, with unquestioning veneration of the orthodox view. His enemies kept it simple—he was evil, furious, and ruthless. One thing was certain: He gave single-minded dedication to any cause he championed and in 1669 he took ownership of Queen Sindeok. Month after month he gathered support, stood before the throne, and argued, explained, cajoled, and badgered for the enshrinement of this queen. The king, in desperation, agreed.

Perhaps the intensity of Song's obsession can be linked directly to two major events in the middle of the 1600s that destabilized his solid, orthodox world. First was the loss of China as Korea's Confucian mentor when the non-Confucian Manchus took over China in 1644, and the second, following closely (1659), was the increasingly divergent views among the scholars that had plunged the court into one of the most violent factional fights on record. Within this unstable environment Song Siyeol fought to sustain the one thing he prized the most—clear, solid adherence to the orthodox expression of beliefs and the rituals that made them tangible. As he looked back to the dynasty's beginning, he saw the glaring lack of proper rites that surrounded their first queen.

Song thus approached the throne in the name of Queen Sindeok, and over the next eight months brought the voices of agreement to a crescendo.

It all began during a normal workday. Every Korean king

functioned as a micromanager and dozens of problems pressed against him daily, many of them of political significance, others seemingly trivial. In each, the king's decision was needed. Every morning the king went to work, most likely in Seonjeongjeon Hall, a small audience chamber in Changdeokgung Palace where he received civil and military officials who sat on both sides of the room according to their rank. A scribe sat in a corner recording the discussions. The king listened to reports and petitions and took part in every detail of running the government.

On this particular day, the fourth day of the first month of 1669, Song Siyeol spoke before the king, moving from land reform to land survey and arguing about how to properly govern the country. The king asked Song Siyeol about murder, and Song quoted Chinese precedent. Next came the subject of marriage between people with the same surname, which Song asked the king to forbid. Next, Song moved forward to address the king saying that they noticed His Majesty had neglected the rituals at the royal ancestral shrine and that it was the king's duty to proceed to Jongmyo Shrine on the first of every month to lead the ceremony. The king responded that he had been ill, and was indeed troubled that he had not carried out the ceremony.[2]

"While we are on the subject"

Seeing his opening, Song Siyeol addressed the subject for which he would become famous. "Now that the subject [of performing ceremonies at Jongmyo Shrine] has come up, and we are discussing proper protocol, it has been on my mind for many months that we must repair the wrongs of the past." And with that innocent statement, he set in motion eight months of discussions before the throne.

Jongmyo Shrine

Having spoken with the king of his sacred obligations of the rituals at Jongmyo Shrine, Song Siyeol kept to that subject of ancestors but brought into it his concern for Queen Sindeok. Showing his personal concern for the founding of the dynasty, he told how some months earlier, he had gone to Gaeseong specifically to look for the home of their founder, King Taejo, and found it definitely in need of royal attention. Now, having spoken of the founder, he moved on to another item from the dynasty's founding that also needed redress.

Song Siyeol reminded the king that Lady Kang had been the royal wife of King Taejo. "After she passed away, all the rituals of the Goryeo Dynasty were followed. At the Buddhist temple they performed ceremonies morning and evening, and it is known that our founding king's affection and sorrow for his beloved queen were so great that he picked up his spoon to eat only after hearing the bell from the temple indicating that the prayers were ascending in her behalf. However, today the treatment of Lady Kang cannot compare with that of King Taejo's other queen, Lady Han. All these years Lady Han has been accorded great honor, in sharp contrast to Lady Kang's treatment. This appears to us to be violating correct protocol. We are not paying appropriate respect!"

The king seemed uninformed, and asked, "While we have been performing royal ceremonies at Jongmyo Shrine, we have never included her, even from the beginning of the dynasty. How did this come about?"

As Song Siyeol elaborated, he moved quickly to the major point of contention—two wives, both legitimate. "I'm truly sorry to lift what I say to your August Body, but during the Goryeo Dynasty the custom was that two wives were legitimate, one wife in the hometown and another wife in the capital. Before King Taejo ascended the throne, he married Lady Kang as his wife in the capital and accorded her all the honors fit for a queen and thus her not being included in Jongmyo Shrine is a regrettable omission and a serious matter. I petition His Majesty to confer with the ministers and include her in Jongmyo Shrine. On my knees this lowly subject dares to appeal to the goodness of the king."

The king responded by saying he would diligently consider the matter and discuss it with cabinet ministers and act on their petition.[3]

Queen Sindeok's Tomb

The next day, the fifth day of the first lunar month, Song Siyeol again knelt before the king, saying, "Truly, we should look at the situation of Queen Sindeok. We must refurbish the tomb and enshrine her spirit tablet in Jongmyo Shrine. This is a critical matter."

The young king entered the conversation by asking how this injustice had come about and Song Siyeol retold the entire story, ending with the events in 1410. When the government honors stopped, he said, they had allowed the family members to perform the tomb rituals, but as time passed, everything had become utterly neglected.

Aware of the need for precedent, Song told the king of a pattern he could follow.

"If you are concerned that your ancestor, King Seonjo, did not restore Queen Sindeok to Jongmyo Shrine in 1581, there is another precedent you might consider, because King Jungjong (r. 1506–1544), the grandfather of King Seonjo, did restore Soreung Royal Tomb, the tomb of King Munjong's wife. One can use this as a model for Lady Kang."

Here, King Hyeonjong had been looking back to 1581 for guidance, whereas Song suggests that he look back even farther to what King Jungjong had done in the early 1500s.[4]

Inspecting the Tomb

Minister of Protocol Yi Jungu went to Jeongneung Royal Tomb to inspect the tomb and reported back, saying that the area lay in ruins. The wall (*gokjang*) was gone. The stone guardians (*seongmul*) were not complete. There were pairs of lanterns, scholar statues (*munseok*), stone columns, and one stone altar. Stone statues of a sheep, tiger, and horse stood on the sides. More than a hundred paces below the tomb mound, a wide area appeared to be the original location of the ceremony rituals. Once a year on Hansik day people did perform ceremonies, but they had to hang a curtain since no memorial hall existed.

Hearing the report, Chief State Councillor Jeong Taehwa and Second State Councillor Heo Jeok (both of the Southern Faction and normally in opposition to Song) advised the king to refurbish the hall and assign a guard to maintain the place.

The king so decreed.

Next, the minister of the Board of War (Byeongjo) reported that, according to protocol, he should assign thirty guards (*ho*) to the tomb, and the king agreed. He ordered that the guards be half from the infantry and half be official tomb guards (*bonneung*). The court appointed supervisors and planned construction of the ritual hall, to begin on the thirteenth day of the third month.[5]

King Taejong's Spirit May Cower before His Father

Song Siyeol let the topic rest for two weeks, and then returned. "King Taejong was a benevolent, wise ruler in every respect but one—that is regarding his treatment of Queen Sindeok. I am convinced that [in the spirit world] the departed soul of our founding king is full of distress and sadness at the way his beloved queen is treated. Even in the midst of wonderful music and vessels full of wine, King Taejong will be full of uncertainty and may even be cowering before his father. Fortunately, because Your Majesty is innately full of genuine filial duty, you can correct this wrong now that you have been informed of it. In the course of honoring your ancestors, you have already ordered the tomb restored. I humbly realize that Your Majesty has a legitimate reason for hesitation, but it is my conviction that there is no reason to hesitate. Once this is done, King Taejo's spirit will be pleased and King Taejong will say, "I have a descendant who has accomplished my intentions."[6]

A week later, Second State Councillor Heo Jeok spoke up. "Ever since I was a child, I have listened to my elders talk about Jeongneung Royal Tomb," thus letting the king know that, outside the court, the story of Queen Sindeok's dishonor was well known among the people, and again letting the king see that opposing factions now agreed.

The Appeals Magnify

The officials from both factions increased their diligence with appeals. Now into the fifth month, many added their voices to that of Song Siyeol. The Board of Restoration (Junggeoncheong), the first counselor from the Office of Special Counselors (Hongmungwan *bujehak*, rank 3A), a reader from the Royal Lectures Office (*sidokgwan*, rank 5A), and the censor-general all presented appeals. Even the Hongmungwan official, Fourth Counselor (*eunggyo,* rank 4A) Nam Iseong, spoke up. "Please, Your Majesty," they begged, "Make a favorable decision!"[7]

Song Jungil, joining his colleague Song Siyeol, took the floor and shifted his argument. "It is the appropriate filial duty to keep the traditions of the ancestors, but it is also our filial duty to complete that which is incomplete. By doing this, you will complete the job of your illustrious ancestors."

A Royal Censorate official, Kim Mangi (*sagan,* rank 3B), modified the argument: "You look on this as a stressful issue, but truly it is a simple thing! If you do this, subsequent kings will follow your example. The righteous anger of the people has reached the heavens. King Taejo in heaven is agitated! You have approved rebuilding the memorial hall, so why do you still refuse Jongmyo Shrine?"

Officials had thus introduced a new idea: The king would be honored for his filial actions if he did enshrine Queen Sindeok into Jongmyo Shrine. But courage was needed to break from past examples—perhaps more courage than King Hyeonjong had at his command. He held fast.

Months passed. The scholars spent hours in the archives searching for old documents, in their rooms preparing petitions, and before the throne presenting arguments. The king must have thought—as had King Seonjo before him—that the officials were wasting their time with their never-ending appeals to goad him into action.

In spite of the king's opposition, however, the Confucian ritualists continued and their arguments were overpowering. They believed to the depths of their souls that because of ritual lapses in the past, Queen Sindeok was unjustly suffering immense pain in her wanderings through space. One day's delay in rectifying the wrongs of the past was one day more in which they, the Confucian supplicants, were "birds and beasts"—a common phrase to describe people who lacked basic moral principles—rather than human beings. The king just as sincerely felt that he could not impose something retroactively that the kings directly concerned at the time (King Taejong and Sejong) had not done. There must have been a reason, King Hyeonjong kept saying, for earlier monarchs to have acted as they did, and he was frankly fearful of enraging the spirits of these royal predecessors.

Unprecedented Unanimity

In the seventh month, Chief State Councillor Jeong Taehwa knelt before the throne with a most unusual statement. "There has never been an issue on which everyone agreed, yet on this one thing— enshrining Queen Sindeok—there is amazing unanimity! Your Majesty must see that this is an important issue."[8]

The king recalled only too clearly the year when the debate over proper rituals had rocked the court, and factional fights had become the epitome of fanatic, contentious behavior. The scholars had torn the court apart with their arguments. And now, just ten years later, these same men came before the king announcing, of all things, unanimity. But the king, ignoring their cohesiveness, answered as usual. "This is a very important matter. I cannot do it lightly."

Day after day, they approached the king with page after page of appeals. Members of the Three Boards took turns. From the Office of Special Counselors (Hongmungwan) came the fourth counselor (eunggyo, rank 4A), the fifth councillor (bugyori, 5B), and the sixth counselor (busuchan, rank 6B). Officials brought in one hundred scholars from the State Archives (Chunchugwan), all experts on

Confucian ritualism.

Finally the king thundered, "There are just too many people in this room! Let only one from each board remain. All others get out!"

They returned, and on this day came two hundred scholars from the Confucian Academy—impressive by their sheer numbers. Huijeongdang Hall in Changdeokgung Palace is fairly small, so it would have been somewhat crowded with only the king and a few officials, plus the scribe in the corner and servants lingering outside. But to add new pressure on the king, the scholars entered one after another until all who were able crowded into the room, with those at the end of the line standing on the stone terrace outside. It was palpably evident that they spoke with one accord.

And yet the king held his ground.[9]

Eighth Month: I Must Be Deliberate

Refusing to give up, on the fifth day of the eighth month the chief state councillor knelt before the king. "We are anxious for Your Majesty to make a decision on this important matter. We are perturbed. The appeal we made is everlastingly correct and appropriate. We are in great frustration. We would like to know why, on this particular matter only, Your Majesty displays such hesitation. We are full of doubt. We humbly appeal that Your Majesty no longer hesitate in correcting this wrong."

And the king, worn down beyond his endurance, announced his decision.

Chapter 12

FINALLY, ENSHRINEMENT

On the fifth day of the eighth month in the tenth year of his reign (1669), King Hyeonjong, in one momentous declaration, broke the grasp of centuries-old precedent and made a decision that no previous monarch had dared to do. He acknowledged Queen Sindeok as a legitimate and rightful queen and declared that as such, she should be properly enshrined in Jongmyo Shrine. Her spirit tablet would take its place beside that of her husband, King Taejo, and his first wife, Queen Sinui.

The news raced through the palace and out into the street. Shouts of rejoicing reverberated like explosive peals of thunder. Officials knelt before their monarch, saying that surely now he could imagine the happiness of his people and know he had done the right thing.

An Avalanche of Activity

Enshrinement—the highest of all Confucian ceremonies—would now become a reality for Queen Sindeok, but proclaiming the news was one thing and making it happen was another. From the modern perspective one might easily disparage the frenetic preparations. The goal, after all, was simply to deposit a twelve-inch piece of wood in a proper niche for safekeeping. But from the perception of seventeenth-century Joseon scholars, the moment the queen's name became inscribed upon that wooden tablet, the tablet became the residence of her royal spirit, and as such required all the preparation, processions, rituals and ceremonies, all the pomp and pageantry, befitting a living queen.

It is impossible to fully comprehend the immensity of the event—the number of people involved, the specific items to be made new, the number of officiates who must learn the embedded number of rituals. The list seemed endless and the available time was short. The king's announcement had been made on the fifth day of the month and rituals at the tomb had to be done on Queen Sindeok's death anniversary, the eleventh day of the same month, allowing just six days in which to prepare. Within that time, the death anniversary had to be certified, the tomb and temple refurbished, all the officials, servants, and military guards and their horses cleaned, groomed, and appropriately attired. The enshrinement into Jongmyo Shrine was supposed to take place on the same day, but everyone acknowledged that would be impossible, given that each of the ceremonies relied on strict adherence to a plethora of details and it simply could not be accomplished in such a short time.[1]

The king appointed Chief State Councillor Jeong Taehwa as head of all ritual ceremonies, and directors of other departments were assigned to supervise completion of the memorial hall at the tomb site and begin preparation for the Jongmyo Shrine enshrinement. Assignments went to the ministers of the Board of Revenue (Hojo) Kim Jwamyeong, the Board of Rites (Yejo) Bak Changwon, and the Board of Works (Gongjo) Yi Minseo.[2]

Jeongneung Royal Tomb and Sinheungam Hermitage

Ceremonial Official (*tongnyewon*) Yi Jungu began planning tomb rituals for the eleventh of the month, but upon examining the ancient records, he found that the queen's actual death anniversary was the thirteenth. With this new information, they gained two workdays and set the date for the tomb ceremony.[3]

On the thirteenth day, officials gathered and proceeded to the tomb. For two hundred years the tomb had lain in various stages of neglect and now, suddenly, officials, soldiers, and their retinue on foot and on horseback made their way from the palace to the village at the base of the hill and on up to the tomb. The king had assigned forty additional troops along with the thirty sent several months earlier to surround the tomb and protect it from wild animals and marauding humans. Surely the villagers in their white farmers' garb gathered in amazement to see such splendor pass through their hamlet, and followed behind, or even ran along the hillside to witness the procession and celebrate the occasion.

Deciding that the Buddhist hermitage was too small and too near the grave site, the king issued a royal decree that it be moved over the hill, enlarged, and renamed Sinheungsa Temple, and that the Buddhist monks be recommissioned to pray for the welfare of Queen Sindeok's spirit.[4] Here again the intertwining of Confucian rituals and Buddhist ceremonies caused no conflict, for each served separate needs—Confucian tomb rituals still depended on Buddhist prayers to guide the spirit into the netherworld.

Jongmyo Shrine

While the ceremony took place at the tomb to the northeast of the city, other officials moved forward with plans to install the spirit tablet in Jongmyo Shrine. Strict observance of the rituals required precision, even to the designated hour for moving an item from one place to another—items could be moved at the hour of the rabbit (five to seven o'clock in the morning), the dragon (seven to nine o'clock), or the snake (nine to eleven o'clock)—and each act called for separate officials and proper ceremony.

The Honorary Name

Before all else, the queen must be given an honorary posthumous name, for this name would be used on her jade book (*okchaek*), her royal seal (*geumbo*), and the new spirit tablet. But ceremonial official Yi Jungu found that no precedent existed for bestowing a retroactive honorary name. His officials searched documents back to the beginning of the dynasty and determined that King Taejo's posthumous name had four syllables, and therefore they decided that Queen Sindeok's name should also have four. They believed King Taejo must have put such a name in her jade book (*sichaek*), but as they could not find it, they settled on the name of Sunwon Hyeonyeong (Gentle Principal Bright Respect).[5]

The Jade Book and Royal Seal

The minister of personnel prepared the jade book—a book literally made of thin pages or strips of jade—on which they could now write Queen Sindeok's posthumous name plus an ode of praise telling of her life and accomplishments. Others carved her name into a golden royal seal. The book and seal were then placed on silk cushions to await the special day. At the appointed time (the hour of the dragon) and with appropriate ceremony, they were taken to Huijeongdang Hall in Changdeokgung Palace to await transfer to Jongmyo Shrine.[6]

The Spirit Tablet

The entire event focused on the queen's spirit tablet, yet that tablet presented the most compelling problem of all. Officials believed that one had been made at her death, but it proved impossible to find. Realizing they must now make a new one, they searched for guidance, yet found nothing.

Planning the tablet. All advice found in the records gave instructions only for repairing damaged tablets, but Queen Sindeok had no original to repair or copy—on their own they must make a completely new one. Regulations explained only that the tablet should be one foot long, carved from either mulberry or chestnut wood, and have a special box built to hold it. The superintendent now recorded all this newly gathered information in the registry of the Superintendent of Repairs (suridogam).[7]

An officer from the Board of Rites reported the next difficulty—the tablet had to be carved at the dwelling place of the spirit, but again they had conflicting information. They found in the records that the original spirit tablet had been left in the Spirit Hall, Inanjeon Hall in Gyeongbokgung Palace, and later taken to the mountain tomb. Now they were unsure where the spirit might dwell—here or there—and thus could not tell where to create the new tablet. Their progress again slowed to a stop.[8]

To break this conundrum, official Song Jungil offered his opinion. "When we look at what Taejo did when Sindeok passed away, we find that the spirit tablet (*sinju wipae*) was returned to Inanjeon Hall, and after three years her portrait scroll (*yeongjeong*) was also placed there. It seems to me that her spirit would have been traveling with the tablet when it was taken to Inanjeon Hall. But this is of little help, because today we do not even know the location of Inanjeon Hall since everything burned a hundred years ago [possibly during the Hideyoshi invasions]. It would seem appropriate to make the new tablet at an existing hall and I suggest we use Euphwadang Hall in Gyeongbokgung Palace."[9]

Adding calligraphy. On the twenty-ninth day, at the assigned hour of the rabbit, the appointed officials with full regalia escorted the tablet to a ceremonial hut (*akcha*) near Gangnyeongjeon Hall in Gyeongbokgung Palace to have the calligraphy written on it. With this task completed, Second State Councillor Heo Jeok performed the ritual required for taking the tablet back to the hall where it had been made, and once there, he performed yet another ritual.[10] The tablet was laid on a blue silk cushion, placed in its container, wrapped with a blue silk covering, and left to await transfer to Jongmyo Shrine.

At that point, the royal seal, the jade book, and the spirit tablet sat ready to be transferred to Jongmyo Shrine, yet no one knew the proper and precise way to get from the palace to the shrine. Thus, one last task remained: to find a precedent they could follow for the actual enshrinement. Designated officials traveled to Ganghwado Island to search through records stored there, and found nothing. The problem was that they must conduct a ceremony for an enshrinement that had been delayed for centuries, and no manual existed for such a thing had never been done before.

A Second Break from Tradition

The scholars asked the king's permission to use their accumulated knowledge to design a completely new manual for this unique ceremony. The king, having no alternative, made his second break from the past and granted permission for the scholars to prepare the manual—and without his knowing, thereby set in motion a new precedent for coming generations.

The Manual of Superintendency for the Transfer of the Spirit Tablet of Queen Sindeok for Enshrinement in Jongmyo Shrine (*Sindeokwanghu bumyodogamuigwe*, 1669)

The manual they developed—the original, complete, handwritten, brown clothbound manual—is extant today and is available to be

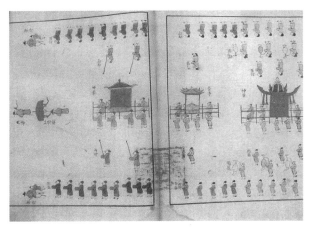

Jongmyo Shrine 1669 Enshrinement Manual: Procession

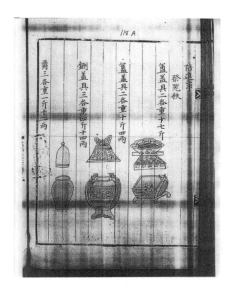

Jongmyo Shrine 1669
Enshrinement Manual:
Implements

viewed where it is stored in the Gyujanggak Royal Library. Once compiled, copies of the manual were placed in widely separate repositories in accordance with the practice for safekeeping of important documents. The first copy went to the king, and additional copies were distributed to Jongmyo Shrine, the State Council (Uijeongbu), the State Archives (Chunchugwan), and the Board of Rites (Yejo), with final copies dispersed to remote temple archives staffed by soldiers and Buddhist monks. One copy each was sent to Ganghwado Island, Taebaeksan Mountain, Odaesan Mountain, and Jeoksangsan Mountain.

Every resource that mentions the ceremony uses only the same five words: "enshrined in Jongmyo Shrine in 1669," leaving the details to one's imagination. But it is those details that make clear and accessible the immensity of the occasion.

Preparation

The manual sets out more than 150 pages of detailed instructions. It lists what had to be prepared, including a table, a chair, and other furniture for the Jongmyo Shrine cubicle; an array of musical instruments; the people in charge, including an official reader; craftsmen, including goldsmiths, silversmiths, painters, and leather workers; and details of what each must produce. These included eight phoenix fans; four golden lanterns; various gold and silver vessels; three more lanterns, one red, one white, and one black; silver and gold stirrups for saddles; ceremonial weapons such as golden axes and gold and silver swords; and ceremonial vessels and their covers. It even specifies the proper inks and brushes to be used to write the manual.

The Day of Transferring

Once all that myriad of ritual items had been prepared, officials were instructed to place them in the ceremonial hut (*akcha*) just outside the spirit-gate on the grounds of Jongmyo Shrine, ready for the official enshrinement the following morning. However, to transfer all the items to that gate, one needed the Great Procession.[11, 12]

The Procession

The day of the Great Procession came on the thirtieth day of the ninth month. At the appointed time (the hour of the snake, from nine to eleven o'clock in the morning) the ceremonial procession left the palace, and it was a procession beyond the imagination. In the manual, detailed drawings cover fourteen pages. More than eighty rows of attendants—325 men—walk two, five, or ten abreast and are clearly labeled as messengers, scribes, military officers, soldiers, archers, musicians, and drummers. Footmen carry poles that support banners, feathered umbrellas, huge fans, gold and silver axes, and gold and silver swords.

In the midst of this grand procession, and guarded on every side, comes the focus of the entire event—five palanquins carried by five sets of footmen. Each elaborately covered box carries one item destined for Jongmyo Shrine: the jade book, the royal seal, special incense. There are two boxes labeled the queen's spirit tablet, but it is said that one was left empty to confuse any evil spirits hovering nearby.[13]

The Day of Enshrinement: 1669, tenth month, first day

The ritual of enshrinement must be conducted without a flaw, and officiates proceeded according to instructions read aloud from the ceremonial book. They carried the spirit tablet across the courtyard, walking on the special gray-green brick walkway (*sillo*) reserved for the spirit. Upon reaching the long, low building with its rows of cinnabar-red pillars, they stopped before the cubicle belonging to King Taejo. Opening the red doors that protected the cubicle, they removed the inner screen and placed Queen Sindeok's spirit tablet in front of the altar. Arranging the specially prepared utensils on the ceremonial table, they continued to follow instructions intoned by the reader and moved through the seven parts of the ceremony. With appropriate kneeling and low bows, they (1) received the spirit; (2) presented food (two soups, three meats, four bowls of rice, five kinds of fruit); (3) offered the first, second, and third cups of wine; (4) received the ancestral blessing; (5) withdrew the table; (6) sent off the spirit; and (7) burned the prayer scroll used in the ceremony.[14]

If the king had officiated, the first of the three cups of wine would be offered by the king himself, but on this day the king said he was not feeling well and could not be present. Perhaps he allowed the enshrinement, but was not completely comfortable with his decision and could not dignify it with his presence.

Approval from Heaven

Suddenly a rainstorm poured down upon the capital and the people cried out that the rain came to wash away the *han* or pathos (*wonhan*) suffered by Queen Sindeok.[15] And then it was over.

Jongmyo Daeje, rite for worshipping the late kings and queens of the Joseon Dynasty in Jongmyo Shrine

After centuries of appeals, hundreds of voices, volumes of arguments, and the frantic flurry of preparations, Queen Sindeok's spirit could settle, finally, into its long-awaited rest.

The prediction made by King Hyeonjong's officials was prescient— the enshrinement took on significance far beyond expectations. As succeeding kings dealt with their own needs to follow precedent when honoring one of their own, they no longer looked back to the ancients, but instead looked to what King Hyeonjong had done in that tenth month of 1669.

Queen Sindeok's enshrinement became the model to emulate.

Part Four

A NAME
REMEMBERED

(1674–2005)

Stele at Queen Sindeok's tomb (Jeongneung Royal Tomb)

Chapter 13

FROM HONOR TO HONORS

The splendid pageantry of 1669 brought a close to Queen Sindeok's controversy, but that which was expected to be the final, culminating restoration of honor instead became the prototype for something entirely new. From 1670 onward, the court no longer looked back to ancient precedents, but instead looked to the enshrinement of Sindeok as the model to follow. What an irony that back near the beginning of this saga King Taejong had made every effort to have her memory disappear and her name forgotten, and now it was Queen Sindeok's name that became the name remembered.

The next four monarchs to mention the queen were connected by their compulsion to rectify injustices against their royal predecessors. Kings in the late 1600s and 1700s worked through the disruption of severe factional shifts and life-changing personal tragedy, while those in the 1800s ruled in name only as their power slid into the grasp of their in-laws, yet all united in their remembrance of Queen Sindeok.

King Sukjong (r. 1674–1720)

King Sukjong's years on the throne were racked by violent factional strife, but in spite of that he accomplished the restoration of much that had lain in ruins since the Japanese and Manchu invasions seventy or eighty years earlier. However, during his first years on the throne he met solid resistance when he attempted to restore posthumous honors to royalty who had been ignored or insulted in the past. Because of the contention between the Southern and Western factions, this king's reign was divided by both time and type of restorations. The time of restorations depended on the faction in power, and all restorations took place only when the Westerners were in power. The type of restorations was also divided. Honors were bestowed on others using Queen Sindeok's ceremony as the model, or honors were given directly to the queen or to her relatives.

Southern Faction's Power: 1674–1680

When King Sukjong took the throne in 1674, the Southerner Heo Jeok had just been appointed chief state councillor, and the king helped the Southern Faction gain power by giving high government positions to Heo Mok and Yun Hyu. With this, the ongoing enmity between the Southern and Western factions, between Song Siyeol and Heo Jeok, turned deadly. Both Song Siyeol and Second State Councillor Kim Suhang were accused of crimes, stripped of their ranks, and sent off into exile (in 1674 and 1675, respectively).

During this time, the court discussed honoring Queen Sindeok by erecting small memorial halls (*bongung*) for her in the towns of Hamheung and Yeongheung on the east coast, where similar halls already existed for her husband, King Taejo. There, with appropriate rituals, they hoped to install additional sets of her spirit tablet (*wipae*), but Heo Jeok, exerting his power as chief state councillor, urged the king to abort these plans, saying that according to Confucian protocol it was not proper to perform rituals at memorial halls.[1] Whether his opposition came from true knowledge or from enmity toward Song Siyeol, who surely would have approved the project, the order was rescinded.

Western Faction Restorations: 1680–1689

Angered by growing dissension within the Southern Faction, King Sukjong brought Westerners Song Siyeol and Kim Suhang back from exile and immediately promoted Kim as chief state councillor (1680). The Westerners then sent Yun Hyu (1680) and Heo Jeok (1682) to their deaths by poison.[2] During these shifts in power, the court resumed plans for royal restorations. They began with the two sons of Queen Sindeok, continued with the second king of the dynasty, and then tackled the most complicated task, finding the grave of Queen Sindeok's father.

The court agreed that each of Sindeok's sons should have been given the posthumous title of grand prince (*daegun*), commensurate with their mother's restored position and consistent with the titles held by the six older sons of their father, King Taejo. King Sukjong granted the request.[3]

A year later the court looked back to the second king of the dynasty who had been pushed aside in 1400 by his younger brother King Taejong. In the chaos of those early years, this man had never received an official royal name. Now, his posthumous title was chosen and he became known as King Jeongjong. Here, for the very first time, officials looked for guidance to the enshrining of Queen Sindeok, noted the great care and precise planning that had gone into her ceremony, and then used this as the model for the neglected monarch.[4]

The third time the queen's name came up, it brought a conundrum. The idea was simple. Officials suggested that since the court had restored Queen Sindeok's honor and elevated her sons, they should also honor her father, Kang Yunseong, by refurbishing his grave. All agreed, but no one knew the location of the grave. The king thus assigned a team to search near the old Goryeo capital of Gaeseong, northwest of Seoul, the area known to have been the Kang family's home. The team did discover a tomb on a knoll near Bupyeong, but the broken cover stone had fallen to the ground and half could not be found. The half that remained had only a partial inscription that showed the title as Great Lord of Sangsan (Sangsan Buwongun) but gave no name. Yi U reported his find to the Royal Genealogy Department (Seonwonbo ijeongcheong) and this office reported to the king. The Board of Rites (Yejo) then assigned workers to prepare a new stone.

On closer inspection, a new problem appeared. The broken stone revealed a date of 1430, indicating that the title "Great Lord of Sangsan" had been bestowed then, and officials knew that the queen's father had received his title from King Hyeonjong in 1669. Clearly this grave belonged to someone else. Work came to a halt, and, not knowing what to do, they waited.[5]

Five months later the magistrate of Gaeseong, An Jin, came forward to say that he remembered a man named Kang Cheonik who lived in Deogwon and claimed to be a direct descendant of Kang Yunseong, Sindeok's father.[6] This same Kang Cheonik had been consulted twelve years prior in 1669 when they had looked for the name of the queen's mother—and now, according to him, Yunseong's grave was right there in Deogwon, cared for and guarded by the Kang family. The stone of this grave was inscribed with the title bestowed by King Hyeonjong in 1669—namely, Lord Gyeongan,

Kang Yunseong. Kang Cheonik explained that Yunseong had had a son, Gyegwon, to whom King Taejong in the early 1400s had given the same honorary title, including Great Lord of Sangsan. Thus the date of 1430 on the grave in Bupyeong must indicate the resting place of the queen's brother, not her father.[7] The king then declared the grave in Deogwon to be that of Queen Sindeok's father, saying that the descendants must know their own ancestor. In the new year, the magistrate of Yeongheung performed proper rituals at the grave.

Song Siyeol continued his need for ritual perfection and discussed the chambers in Jongmyo Shrine, saying that some spirit tablets had many words while others had few. The king countered by saying that nothing had been done in the past, so he objected to doing anything now. However, he summoned his advisors of rank two and above, and they agreed that this negligence should be corrected, but in order to install the new titles they must have proper rituals. Again they chose to emulate Queen Sindeok and follow the 1669 manual.[8]

Southern Faction's Return: 1689–1694

The Southerners moved back into power for another six years, and their enmity with the Westerners now turned deadly. Song Siyeol was exiled, and as he walked, the king's messengers overtook him to present him with the royal poison. Kim Suhang's exile sent him to a small island far from the capital, but there he also was forced to take poison.

Western Faction's Power

The Western Faction regained power in 1694, picking up where it had left off even without its famous leaders.

The court reconsidered the idea of placing memorial halls for Queen Sindeok in Hamheung and Yeongheung, and this time the king approved the request. Eulogies (*jemun*) were hung in both halls, and appropriate ceremonies took place on the nineteenth and twenty-eighth days of the twelfth month of 1695.

Another request that had been rejected earlier was an effort to restore the proper title to Prince Nosan, the child-king who some three hundred years earlier had met with treachery from within his own family. Now using Queen Sindeok's enshrinement manual for the third time, the court moved to give this king-demoted-to-prince a royal title. King Sukjong asked advice from a group of 491 scholars, all of whom attended the meeting, and with that, Prince Nosan received the posthumous name of Great King Danjong (Danjong Daewang). In making the restored king's new spirit tablets they again, for the third time, followed Queen Sindeok's manual and also celebrated with a special civil service exam (*gwageo*) as had been done when they installed Queen Sindeok.[9]

Thus during King Sukjong's reign, and only with the Western Faction in power, Queen Sindeok's name came before the throne seven separate times. Her ceremony was used to provide the second king of the dynasty with his official title as King Jeongjong, repair inconsistencies in the Jongmyo Shrine, and elevate Prince Nosan to his position as King Danjong. For Queen Sindeok and her family, the king elevated each of her murdered sons to the position of Grand Prince, refurbished the grave of her father, and placed her spirit tablets in Hamheung and Yeongheung. With this, her name disappeared until a dream spurred King Jeongjo into action.

King Jeongjo (r. 1776–1800)

When King Jeongjo ascended the throne, he began a long reign with strong leadership that made him one of the most respected of monarchs. A scholar equal to any, he established the Gyujanggak Royal Library and research center and encouraged the study and writing of history, geography, botany, and astronomy. During these years, many Korean historians shifted away from their study of Chinese history and instead began documenting the history of Korea. One such historian was Yi Geung-ik (1736–1806), whose unofficial history *Yeollyeosil gisul* has often been consulted for the present volume.

King Jeongjo's care of his ancestors began at once. Within ten days of ascending the throne, the king conferred on his father, who had died while still crown prince, the posthumous title Crown Prince Jangheon and then regularly visited his father's grave. In addition, he determined to visit the tomb of every king and queen of the dynasty, and according to his biographer, Yi Mansu, during the twenty-four years of his reign he made seventy visits to the royal tombs.[10] Queen Sindeok's name came to his attention three times, causing him to care for the memorial halls and place a stele at her birthplace.

Fifteen years into his reign, King Jeongjo sent Seo Yeongbo, an official of the Gyujanggak Royal Library, to Hamheung and Yeongheung to inspect the memorial halls. Seo reported that the rituals and the items used for the ceremonies were inconsistent, and the king responded that they must forbid such improper rituals. He forbade them buying anything from the market in Seoul. "When we added Queen Sindeok's hall during King Sukjong's reign," said the king, "Minister Yi was governor of the province, and he presided over the two memorial halls. His actions [for Queen Sindeok] must be used as the precedent. He used only items from his own area, not from Seoul, to do the ceremony. Continue this way."[11]

Next, a scholar made an appeal to honor King Taejo's own ancestors, who were also enshrined in Yeongheung. King Taejo's father, he admitted, had been only a general, yet in the practice of honoring four ancestors, he had been given the honorary title of "Great King" (Hwanjo Daewang), and his tablets had been enshrined, yet no follow-up rituals had been done. Again the problem seemed to be what to do for the spirit of someone so many centuries after death. The king hesitated.

The next day the king made a startling announcement. During the night the spirit of his ancestor high in heaven came to him in a dream and gave him instructions. "I have wanted always to honor my ancestors, and from the dream I came to understand that we should do no less for the Great King Hwanjo than what was done for Queen Sindeok."

Now for the fourth time, a king ordered the officials to follow what King Sukjong had done for Queen Sindeok in 1695, and do the same for the Great King Hwanjo and his wife. With that, he ordered an elaborate celebration for the memorial halls on the east coast.[12]

In 1799 the king again summoned Seo Yongbo, now the minister of the Board of Rites, to discuss the condition of all royal tombs. At the mention of Jeongneung Royal Tomb, Queen Sindeok's tomb, an official spoke up to remind the court that the anniversary of her birth was near, and perhaps they should erect a memorial stone (*biseok*) at her birthplace. King Jeongjo readily approved, but they faced the usual problem—they had to find the site.

An official remembered the story of King Taejo meeting Lady Kang at a well near her home and he spoke up. "We know that her father's hometown was Sangsan, also called Goksan. Old chronicles tell us that the queen (before she was queen, of course) presented King Taejo with a cup of water from the creek with willow leaves floating on top so that he would not drink too fast. The creek where they met was called Yongyeon (Dragon Pond) and it flowed at the foot of a peak called Yongbong (Dragon Peak). I have heard that beside that creek still stand a few ruins of the former buildings. If these two names continue, we should be able to determine Queen Sindeok's birthplace."[13]

The king sent officials to the local town to make inquiries among the elderly citizens in the neighborhood. The men reported back saying they had summoned citizens surnamed Kang and had been told that a short distance east of Goksan was the cornerstone of the house in which Lady Kang's father had lived. Even today, the locals said, the foundation stone and creek still existed. Upon hearing this, the team hurried to the location, followed by the mayor of Goksan, several elderly citizens, and the Kang relatives. They inspected the site and indeed, there was a small hill called Sillyusan Mountain, and at the foot of that, facing east, was the original site of the house of Lady Kang's father. Nearby the water still rushed from the mountain, slowed into a pond, and then flowed east to become a creek. Whether the names were still Dragon Pond and Dragon Peak it was difficult to ascertain, but there surely was a peak and a river. The king replied that, although the reports were not complete, it did seem believable that the site mentioned was the correct place, for it agreed with what was written in various unofficial histories. The king decreed they should erect a memorial monument on the site of the foundation stone that the locals had shown them near her birthplace in Goksan, and he would personally write the memorial to be carved onto the stele (*biseok*).

During the final years of King Jeongjo's long reign, Queen Sindeok's name had come before the throne twice as the king cared for the memorial halls and her birthplace. The next mention of the queen came during the reign of King Sunjo, where again the court adhered to the rituals used in 1669. The final time her name came up, it came with an unexpected twist.

King Sunjo (r. 1800–1834)

Sunjo took the throne at age ten with the Queen Dowager as regent, and within five years Queen Sindeok's name surfaced as the court dealt with the recurrence of the same vexing problem—how to be utterly precise with rituals that affected the spirit world.

Even in the 1800s, scholars still fixated on proper and exact details. Here in 1804 they pondered whether certain rites at a tomb might properly be done before or after the actual death anniversary. After the necessary perusal of records, the court found thirteen occasions on which the ceremony had been conducted early, and they found a ritual for Queen Sindeok that had taken place a full six months in advance.

"So we humbly believe," said the official, "that auspicious rituals can be done ahead of time. This is the precedent that we find with Queen Sindeok and with others."[14]

A strange turn of events took place in 1824 when the magistrate of Hamgyeong-do province, Nam Yi-ik, was doing the annual inspection of royal sites. He reported that he had heard rustling inside Queen Sindeok's shrine at Yeongheung. "We moved everything and still heard the squeak, so we dared to look into Queen Sindeok's memorial chest. When we opened the chest, we noticed that the two characters

'Kang ssi' (of Kang Clan) on her spirit tablet were worn off."

The king dispatched cabinet minister Bak Jonghun to check all the tablets and this official reported that the characters were made with India ink and looked new. He felt no need for repairs. The cover of the tablet chest opened and closed properly, and the front and back were joined well. The king, apparently not questioning the discrepancy of opinions, decreed that Governor Nam had made a mistake by acting rashly and he should be dismissed and sent off into exile![15] One wonders why the king did not question the completely different answers.

Lady Han Is Remembered: 1824

After 150 years of references to Queen Sindeok, a descendant of the Han family approached the throne requesting honor for his ancestor, Lady Han/Queen Sinui. Han Cheolje appealed to the king, saying that her birthplace had no stele. Using the precedent accorded Queen Sindeok in 1799 when King Jeongjo ordered a memorial stone erected to mark Queen Sindeok's birthplace, the court agreed to do the same for Queen Sinui. This woman had not lived to experience the new dynasty, they said, but she had been mother to six sons who later became princes and kings. Although her spirit tablet rested in Jongmyo Shrine, a stele had never been erected at her birthplace. The king agreed that this was a grave oversight and ordered that the stone monument with proper inscription be put in place.[16]

It is perhaps fitting that this final use of Queen Sindeok's ceremony brought recognition to Lady Han/Queen Sinui, the one who had unwittingly caused Queen Sindeok's dishonor. These two, who had begun the dynasty together so many years ago, now met again near the dynasty's close as if some heavenly mandate had brought their spirits face to face. In both the tangible and spirit worlds, this action by the court gave a final closure to the disparity between these two women. Having in 1669 become equals in the royal world of Jongmyo Shrine, here in 1824 they are taken back to their beginnings and the cycle is closed as Lady Han's birthplace is made equal to that of Lady Kang.

Chapter 14

INTO THE TWENTIETH CENTURY

The final hundred years of the Yi royal house limped along in name only, for circumstances presented the court with a line of four child-kings, one after another whose mother or father then ruled as regent. The four kings who began their reigns as children (and their accession ages) were King Sunjo, age ten (r. 1800–1834); King Heonjong, age seven (r. 1834–1849); King Cheoljong, age eighteen, older but equally unprepared (r. 1849–1863); and King Gojong, age eleven (r. 1863–1907).

When King Gojong took the throne (r. 1863–1907), his father (Prince Regent Heungseon Daewongun) acted as his regent, quickly took control of the court, and worked his way through many restorations, three of which happened to be significant to Queen Sindeok. First, for Sinheungam Hermitage northeast of Seoul, he changed the name back to Heungcheonsa Temple in honor of the original building and personally wrote the calligraphy for the hanging board to announce the temple's new name. Next, in 1889, finding that some rooms in the Jongmyo Shrine had memorial jade books with a special name on them and some did not, the king ordered the characters "Jeolbi" be added to the jade books of all queens. And finally, in 1900, when the king found that Queen Sindeok's tomb at Jeongneung Royal Tomb lacked a stele, he ordered a monument stone prepared and in his own calligraphy he wrote the epitaph to be inscribed on both front and back of the tall stone.[1]

The front side of the tombstone bears the inscription "Daehan Sindeok Gohwanghu Jeongneung (大韓 神德高皇后貞陵)," which means "Jeongneung Royal Tomb of Empress Sindeok of the Korean Empire."

A Cataclysmic Rift: 1910–1953

A chasm, deep and dark, now swallows—for the purpose of staying focused on the queen—the next sixty years of Korean history. The chasm holds Korea as a colony of Japan (1910–1945), the division of the peninsula (1945), the establishment of two separate governments in 1948 (the communist Democratic People's Republic of Korea in the north and the democratic Republic of Korea in the south), and the devastating Korean War (1950–1953). Readers wishing to know more about these years may like to read Bruce Cumings's *Korea's Place in the Sun*, which devotes several chapters to these years.

Picking Up, Moving Forward
The Four Significant Sites

After years of turmoil, the southern half of the peninsula—the newly formed Republic of Korea—caught its collective breath and began to forge ahead constructing its own history. Now the Korean government in the south put its energy into modern ways of functioning. Recovery dominated the 1950s and 1960s, and in the 1970s efforts went into exploring and restoring both archaeological and historical sites.

The Cultural Heritage Administration took over maintenance of all historic shrines, palaces, and tombs, and the first two objectives in its charter directly impacted Queen Sindeok's story. The first item states that properties must be preserved in their original condition; the second states that the properties, as well as their surroundings, must be protected from indiscriminate development. Both these guidelines are reflected in the four significant sites that entered Queen Sindeok's story between 1396 and 1400—Jongmyo Shrine, Heungcheonsa Temple, her tomb, and her tombstones. All four, five when including the great bronze bell, have survived the wars and remain intact to this day. Since each site is accessible and welcomes visitors, they are presented here in the order of a walk around Seoul.

Jongmyo Shrine

Jongmyo Shrine received its own honors when in 1995 UNESCO listed it as a World Heritage site, and in 2001 designated the ritual and dance used in the ceremony as a Masterpiece of the Oral and Intangible Heritage of Humanity. The musicians who play the ancient instruments are themselves members of the contemporary reincarnation of the Royal Court Music Academy, now called the National Music Academy (Cultural Intangible Treasure no. 1, Gugakwon). The Jeonju Yi clan—those descendants of Yi Seonggye— conduct a yearly ceremony at the shrine on the first Sunday in May, and to prepare for the ceremony, the participants attend a rigorous training program using *Jeollye gyoyuk yeonsu gyojae* (Instruction Manual for Rituals at Jongmyo Shrine).

Outside Jongmyo Shrine's main hall, the explanation board clearly indicates that the first room belongs to King Taejo and both his queens, Sinui and Sindeok, providing a close-up view of "one part of an immense, unbroken stream that has flowed over this scene" for hundreds of years.[2]

The Great Bronze Bell

An invigorating walk to the west of Jongmyo Shrine takes one to Deoksugung Palace and the great bronze bell cast for Queen Sindeok in 1462. According to the description board in front of the bell, Grand Prince Hyoryeong, the second son of King Taejong, petitioned it specifically in memory of Queen Sindeok and had it hung in the courtyard of the original Heungcheonsa Temple. It seems appropriate that after years of moving from place to place around Seoul, the bell has come to rest in the courtyard of this small palace, bringing it as near as possible to the site of the original temple.

Heungcheonsa Temple

A fire in 1510 destroyed the temple built for Queen Sindeok in downtown Seoul and it was never restored. The current temple by that name is tucked away in the hills of northeast Seoul in the Donam-dong district, halfway up Arirang Hill. Originally dedicated as a prayer temple for Queen Sindeok's departed spirit, one wonders about such rituals today, and Robert Buswell, who spent some time in a monastery, tells us that this seeming ubiquity of ritual is a bit deceptive, with only a few monks directly involved in the majority of ceremonies. One or two ritual specialists perform the whole ceremony entirely on their own, without any audience at all. Ritual is commonly perceived as lower on the hierarchy of religious vocations than either meditation or doctrinal study, ranking about on a par with administration.[3] One wonders if the monks ever think of Queen Sindeok—perhaps only when a random visitor comes mentioning her name.

Jeongneung Royal Tomb

Not far from the temple, and somewhat easier to find, is the royal tomb. It still takes a spirit of exploration to hike from the subway station up through the labyrinth of small neighborhood streets and alleys to come to the gate of Jeongneung, but once there, one sees the implementation of the Cultural Heritage Administration's guidelines—to keep sites in their original condition. The tomb looks as unfinished today as it did in 1409. On top of the hill, the grave mound is not encircled by the usual huge stone hedge and the only stone sculptures are a sheep, tiger, civil servant, horse, an altar table, and of course the Goryeo-style lantern. At the base of the hill stand the small ceremonial building and the hut that houses the King Gojong stele. The standard red gate marks off the sacred enclosure.

In the 1970s all royal tombs in South Korea were elevated to official Historic Sites. Queen Sindeok's tomb, Jeongneung Royal Tomb (three miles northeast of downtown Seoul), became Historic Site no. 208 and King Taejo's tomb, Geonwonneung Royal Tomb (ten miles northeast of Seoul), became Site no. 193. (Queen Sinui's tomb received no such designation, for it remains in North Korea in Ji-dong, Gaepung-gun, near Gaeseong.) Here at the tomb, as with the Ancestor Shrine, the government is responsible for the upkeep of the grounds, while the Jeonju Yi family is responsible for the annual ritual. In 1972 it was determined that each of the fifty-one Joseon royal tombs should be honored directly by the descendants of the kings and queens buried there. Appropriately, Jeongneung Royal Tomb was assigned to descendants of Grand Prince Gwangpyeong, that fifth son King Sejong gave in adoption to the widow of the murdered Grand Prince Muan back in the early 1400s precisely so that there would be descendants to perform the rites. These descendants have resumed their designated task with an annual incense ceremony (*jehyang*) on a fixed date of September 23 by the solar calendar. As with Jongmyo Shrine, the participants follow detailed instructions for each officiate, including Overseer, Presenting Officials, Master of Ceremonies, Grand Marshall, Right Incense, Left Incense, and Incense Fire Lighter.[4] The parklike grounds are lovely, a creek meanders through it, and visitors who maintain the quiet solemnity of the site are welcome.

The Neglected Tombstones

Finally, as the twenty-first century began, a long-ignored and possibly forgotten incident from 1410 became part of Queen Sindeok's final rectification. Her magnificent tombstones, once obliterated in the banks of a river, became rescued and sanctified in the walls of a cosmopolitan parkway—her one final, unique, and utterly public honor. These stones, and the waterway that became their home for six hundred years, have a story of their own that parallels that of the queen.

Chapter 15

TOMBSTONES WITHOUT A TOMB

Queen Sindeok's final honor is an ultimate, purely personal, totally public honor that takes us again to those tombstones that became detached from the tomb they were carved to protect. Queen Sindeok's story has moved in the esoteric realm of spirits, spirit tablets, words, and rhetoric. The tombstones now present a tangible, visible, and solid echo of the queen's saga. The stones began, as did the queen, with the highest of honors. When the queen died in 1396, King Taejo hired master stonemasons to do the intricate carvings and called the governor of Jejudo Island to attend as overseer. The finished stones surrounded the tomb, sharing the honor of their queen. Then, as the queen's honors were stripped away, so the stones moved from tomb to dump heap to muddy riverbank to the gloom submerged under a roadway and finally to the filth of a sewer channel. In 2005, some six hundred years later, the stones were released from the dark and received their ultimate honor.

The Stream and Gwangtonggyo Bridge

Cheonggyecheon Stream cuts across the center of Seoul from west to east and flows on into the Hangang River. In the past this stream was a key waterway supplying cooking water, washing water, a playground for children, and yes, carrying away the sewage. Its banks offered home to ancient settlers and, more recently, to post–Korean War refugee squatters.

The early bridges across the stream were made only of wood, and frequent flooding often washed them away. In the seventh month of 1410, the year after Queen Sindeok's tomb had been moved from the city, major floods predictably collapsed the bridges. This time, the royal governing board asked the king for permission to convert Gwangtonggyo Bridge—the main bridge that stood slightly southeast of Gyeongbokgung Palace—from wood to stone. The king gave permission and Gwangtonggyo Bridge gained importance as the first stone bridge in the city. The first and most immediate task was to shore up the muddy banks of the stream to support the weight of the new bridge. Workers chose to use the enormous hedge stones left behind from the tomb of Queen Sindeok. Whether the king ordered this or workmen simply took the best that was available will never be known, but it is sometimes said that the political rivalry between King Taejong and Queen Sindeok resulted in her tombstones being used to support the bridge, thus forcing common people and their animals to walk over them, an ultimate insult to a royal memory.[1]

Over time, the stream continued to flood, spreading filth, disease, and a high mortality rate along its banks. Isabella Bird Bishop, visiting Seoul in 1894, described it thusly:

> "One of the 'sights' of Seoul is the stream or drain or watercourse, a wide, walled, open conduit, along which a dark-colored festering stream slowly drags its malodorous length, among manure and refuse heaps which cover up most of what was once its shingly bed. [One sees] women of the poorest class, some ladling into pails the

compound which passes for water, and others washing clothes in the fetid pools which pass for a stream."[2]

The Roadway

The blight of Cheonggyecheon Stream demanded attention, and talks were held as early as 1895 and again in 1926 but came to naught. When the Korean War ended in 1953, refugees crowded along the stream creating a shanty town of poverty, squalor, and rampant crime. Determined to make a change, officials cleaned the area, covered the stream, and created a roadway to ease the new and increasing traffic congestion. Gwangtonggyo Bridge remained in place, but in order to lay the roadway over it, the railings were removed and stored on the grounds of Changgyeonggung Palace.[3] Three years later, in 1958, the *JoongAng Ilbo* newspaper sent a team of reporters underground to photograph the sewer pipe that had been cut through Queen Sindeok's tombstones, and the situation of these historic stones came briefly into public view. After that, the roadway took shape above the sewer, until finally the stream was completely covered. The relics from the monarchy lay forgotten beneath the modern highway.

Transformation

New life for the stream, the bridge, and the stones began twenty years later as part of the six hundredth anniversary of the founding of Seoul.

In 1994 Seoul came alive with plans to celebrate its six hundredth anniversary. Officials at the Chohung Bank in the center of town recalled that the street in front of the bank had once been a river and the ancient Gwangtonggyo Bridge had been right there at the crossroads. As their contribution to Seoul's anniversary, they decided to construct a one-quarter scale model of the bridge and place it on the front corner of their office building, thus bringing to public consciousness the history hidden below ground. Appropriately clad in rubber overalls, workers and photographers descended into the sewer to find the bridge and in so doing found, cleaned, and photographed the tombstones that still supported the bridge. The team brought all this research together in a booklet, *Gwangtonggyo Bridge, Joseon's Premier Bridge* (*Gwangtonggyo, Joseonui jeil dari*).

Queen Sindeok's story began its return. "Times change and as they do, people look back on the past and reinterpret events and ideas. Often the debate focuses on place—the actual site of an event—and whether it deserves to be remembered or forgotten."[4]

In 1994, during the height of Seoul's six-hundred-year anniversary celebrations, and perhaps prompted by the work of the Chohung Bank, the *JoongAng Ilbo* again ran the 1958 photo of Queen Sindeok's tombstone in the sewer.[5] About the same time, several people began seriously considering the plight of dilapidated neighborhoods that hugged the route of the expressway above the covered stream. Venturing down into the sewer, they saw the underside of Gwangtonggyo Bridge still standing there in the dark and began to explore ideas that might get rid of the roadway and bring back the stream and with it the bridge and Queen Sindeok's tombstones. When Lee Myung-bak became mayor of Seoul in 2002, he spearheaded a project to restore the stream.

The vision expanded. Within a year (July 1, 2003), workers began demolishing the highway and exposing the original streambed. They diverted the sewer and pumped in recycled water to keep the stream flowing. By July 2005 they had created an uninterrupted parkway running through the center of Seoul—an instant tourist attraction. The stream is now bordered by walkways and plants both wild and tame, plus multileveled decks and terraces along the banks that invite people to sit and relax. Multiple arrangements of rocks below the water create a variety of white-water patterns, while mixed arrangements of stepping-stones above water add multiple ways for the more adventurous to cross over the stream. One sees families and shoppers strolling, children leaping across the stones, others sitting and relaxing, all reveling in the totally new gathering place for the ancient city.

The Tombstones

During excavation of the stream, workers uncovered three ancient bridges and, following preservation guidelines, they restored two of the bridges right where they found them, in their original location. The third, Gwangtonggyo Bridge, was moved slightly upstream, because its original position had become a major traffic thoroughfare. In cleaning the stones supporting Gwangtonggyo Bridge, workers realized they had found all twelve of the major stones from Queen Sindeok's tomb, plus many smaller connectors and cornerstones—some damaged, many in near perfect condition. The bridge was then reconstructed exactly as it had been found, including its stone foundations, embankments, and underwater paving stones. The intricately carved hedge stones were cleaned and set in the wall to support the bridge. People passing by stop to look, perhaps unaware of the full tragedy of the tomb these stones were carved to protect.

Thus, after years of dishonor, Queen Sindeok's tombstones are now on permanent display, in the very public walls of the parkway of Cheonggyecheon Stream in downtown Seoul. No other queen has suffered so long, in so many separate venues, and no other has been vindicated in such a thoroughly prominent display. In 1396 her devoted husband, King Taejo, commissioned the guardian generals to surround her tomb in the center of Seoul, and now after all that she and the spirit-generals have been through, the circle has closed as the stones stand once more in the center of the city.

Worker cleaning tombstones in sewer (top)

Cheonggyecheon Parkway after Cheonggyecheon Stream restoration project, 2017 (bottom)

Chapter 16

REFLECTIONS

One seemingly simple problem—restoring honor and status to a long-deceased queen—continued to vex kings, scholars, and commoners alike through more than five centuries. This current attempt to record and make sense of such a vast, ancient, and dramatic problem has forced us to look in some detail at the ever-changing scene of Korean history. In tracking the controversies that raged over Queen Sindeok, we have been introduced to problems faced by the monarchy, changes in Korean neo-Confucianism, renovations in the city of Seoul, and modern institutions that carry on the royal legacy. Along the way, we have seen vignettes from the lives of many who acted for or against this queen. Now stopping to reflect on the story, I have chosen the words carefully: we have "seen" vignettes and been "introduced" to their problems but we remain visitors in a foreign country. We use words, aware that they may not mean today what they meant then. We make an effort to comprehend, aware that we are yet missing the depth and complexities of emotions that fueled the long-gone actors in the story. We proceed the best we can.

This book purports to tell of a young Korean queen, yet almost no trustworthy detail survives. Royal rhetoric would have us believe she was beautiful, intelligent, and well loved by her husband. This may or may not be true. There are, however, a few facts. She was the first queen of the Joseon Dynasty. She took ill and died in 1396. After death she suffered multiple dishonors, and if all had gone as planned, she would have been forgotten. Beyond that, her story became the story of each person, royal or not, who mentioned her name from the beginning of the dynasty to the present day. Because of her, we have glimpsed the famous—kings and scholars, rogues and near-saints—and the unknowns who appeared out of nowhere to take up her cause. The story has been the attempt to understand those who dealt with the problem and its ultimate resolution.

Upon reflection, there emerges a group of "unknowns" that we must now recognize and credit—a group that has passed by unnoticed. These unknowns are the scholars who thought out, organized, and wrote that 1669 manual of enshrinement. As each succeeding king turned to "Queen Sindeok" as the precedent to follow, it was, of course, not the queen but the manual that they turned to, and thus all those unnamed scholars were honored by the choice. They are the ones who worked furiously over such a short period of time to pool their knowledge and produce a manual of such precision and clarity that "Queen Sindeok's manual" was the precedent to follow. We are left with no way to honor those scholars other than to appreciate their work.

The Joseon Dynasty began with the establishment of the Yi clan as the royal family, and we have seen the major problems that precipitated Queen Sindeok's dishonor—royal succession, the overwhelming need for royal precedent, the fear of making a royal error. Some may have used Confucianism as a shield, but clearly, belief in Confucian teachings galvanized certain kings to be the most dedicated of sovereigns. In watching these men, we have been bombarded with the never-ending minutiae of Confucian teaching—correct rituals, the care of tombs, the specifications for spirit tablets, memorial halls, and steles. We reflect, and still wonder, at the amount of thought, energy, and above all delay, that went into much of their daily work.

However, Queen Sindeok's story did not end when both royalty and Confucian practices became obsolete. We have visited her four significant sites and found them intact, cared for, and hosting ceremonies in the same form and from the same manuals as was done in the past. We have come across the institutions that carry on, such as the National Music Academy, the Cultural Heritage Association, and, on several levels, the Jeonju Yi family royal clan. We reflect on the men at the Jongmyo Shrine ritual and the tomb ritual who come to take part in a tradition and honor a legacy set in motion by their ancestors. These men are not college students in search of summer employment. The ceremonies are not tourist attractions. The men are direct descendants of the Yi family kings and they come together to claim solidarity as descendants of an ancient family.

Commonalities

Having looked at uncountable pages of detail, one must ask what, if anything, all these people had in common. Why is it that these particular people entered the story? Their expressed motives differ greatly—kings hampered by succession problems and fear of portents, spirits, and the manifest correctness of predecessors; scholars striving for correct ritual adherence or personal power. These are the facts, the details.

But there appears something more. Beyond the details lurk passion, determination, and men with beliefs so strong they were willing to die, to kill, to hold out against the mob, to believe that a wrong should be made right, item by item, century after century. Each person looked at something long gone and concluded it was still not right. Each had the determination to make revision happen. And their passion made a change for Queen Sindeok.

Through it all, this queen has remained unique. Other queens had their status revoked, but their restoration, once accomplished, was complete, final, and forgotten. Queen Sindeok's situation came and went and came again. Each appearance of her name was powered by different situations and different people, so that her story has become the story of the people who, with palpable determination, orchestrated her dishonor, debated her rise and fall, and, one by one, restored, renovated, and preserved her status and that of her four significant sites. That her name continues to surface even today highlights the longevity of Koreans' respect for the past and the closeness with which they hold their history. As Helen of Troy was said to be the face that launched a thousand ships, Korea's Queen Sindeok is a name that sparked a thousand arguments, pleas, and refusals.

They say that a spirit roams, restless, until it has a proper resting place. For this queen, finally, her spirit tablet rests in Jongmyo Shrine, her tomb is watched over and cared for, the temple reveres her name, and the tombstones have risen from the sewer to stand as spirit-generals aboveground more clearly and publicly than could ever have been imagined. Queen Sindeok's honor, status, and significant sites are now restored.

May she rest in peace.

Epilogue

I AM INTRODUCED TO THE QUEEN

Incense smoke and candle smoke mingled with the words of the old woman as she introduced me to the spirit of Queen Sindeok. On a perfectly normal afternoon, a single word had pulled me through an invisible barrier from the polite public world into another, hidden world, one seen by invitation only.

My husband and I had been sitting under the trees across the stream from Queen Sindeok's tomb, listening to an old woman we knew only as Han Halmeoni, Grandmother Han, finish her story. We had been here before, but her unique story drew us back for a second visit. She appeared to be nothing more than a little old woman running a snack shop for visitors to the tomb area—and so she was, with one difference: She had come to the tomb more than forty years earlier at the direct invitation of the long-dead queen.

In the 1950s, the Korean War had robbed her of her husband, her son, and her health. Only thirty-one years old, she was ill and expected to die. Then came the vision.

A beautiful woman dressed in the silk robes of ancient royalty awoke her in the middle of the night, demanding obedience and promising, in exchange, a return to health.

"I am Queen Sindeok of the family Kang," the vision said. "My grave is untended and I cannot rest. You are of the Han family, the family that caused all my troubles. I beg you to serve me now and for the rest of your life.

"You think you are dying, but if you will care for my spirit and my grave, I will bless the water that flows near the tomb.

"Come," she said. "Be my hands and feet. Drink the water. I will cure you."

The vision faded.

No one believed her story, of course. Her parents thought she had gone mad and committed her to a mental hospital, but the doctors concluded she was quite sane, except that, indeed, she had seen a vision. With that, her parents, hoping it would restore her health as the vision had promised, gave her permission to find the grave site and tend the tomb.

Every week, dressed in the long white clothing still worn in the 1950s, she took a bus to the foot of the mountain, walked through the village, ignored the taunts, and climbed the hill. Week after week she swept the derelict buildings at the base of the hill, pulled weeds from the knoll that housed the tomb, and drank the water that flowed there. Finally she had a small house built right beside the stream at the foot of the queen's hill. A lonely place in those days, she said. But she tended the spirit, drank the water, grew strong, and has remained healthy in the spirit's (apparent) care for more than forty years.

We had returned to ask her just how she went about "caring" for the queen, and since this was our second visit with her, she felt familiar and talked freely.

"I keep this tiny shop and live in a room in the back. I have an altar to the queen in a narrow hallway between my room and the shop, and there I bow and talk to her, giving thanks every day. On the first and fifteenth of each month I take a food offering down to the spring. I do it at night now, because of the tourists, and also because the park attendants frown on it. I also light incense there."

All this time, as we sat listening to her long and detailed story, she paid no attention to me, a foreigner—she told her story to my husband. But suddenly she stopped and stared intently at my husband.

"You say you are a Kang?"

"Yes."

"Then you are related to the queen!"

"Yes."

She turned, and for the first time looked directly at me.

"You are his wife! Then you are also a Kang. Come! I will introduce you to the queen!"

She sprang up, expecting me to follow.

My breath caught; my mind whirled.

Puzzled, I stood, walked out of my Western logic, and stepped into the hidden world of the spirits.

Grandmother Han darted around behind the store and opened a door into the hallway that separated the store from her residence. At the end of the hall stood the altar of her own creation. The lower shelf held two candles and an incense burner. On a higher shelf sat the spirit tablet contained in a chest of polished wood. Opening the doors of the small box, she exposed the wooden tablet carved with Queen Sindeok's name. Carefully, she lit the incense, then the candles, and waited as the smoke rose to encircle the spirit tablet.

Then she turned and pushed me forward.

"*Insahaseyo.* Make a greeting!"

How does one greet an unseen spirit—a royal spirit? What ceremony have I walked into—shamanistic? Certainly not Confucian, or even Buddhist. Mentally grasping for correctness—for the sake of Han Halmeoni if not for the unseen queen—I stepped forward and put my palms together, braced against my chest, thinking, "one bow to a monk, three bows to Buddha"—and concluded that two might do for a queen.

Satisfied, she pushed me aside, turned back to the altar, and began mumbling softly to the queen in royal honorifics. I caught some phrases: "from far away ... new to your family ... wants to meet you ... a book." On and on she talked, lost in her own spirit world, her voice becoming more and more excited. Suddenly she turned away from the altar, circled around me with eyes seeing nothing, patted me on the head and shoulders, and continued talking to the queen.

I began to worry. *What happens next? Where is my husband? Surely if this gets out of control, he will rescue me!*

And then, as suddenly as she had begun, she stopped, blew out the candles, and closed the door to the spirit tablet.

I had been formally introduced to the queen.

APPENDIX

Appendix 1

Kings of the Joseon Dynasty, 1392–1910

*1. King Taejo 태조 太祖	r. 1392–1398
*2. King Jeongjong 정종 定宗	r. 1398–1400
*3. King Taejong 태종 太宗	r. 1400–1418
*4. King Sejong 세종 世宗	r. 1418–1450
5. King Munjong 문종 文宗	r. 1450–1452
6. King Danjong 단종 端宗	r. 1452–1455
*7. King Sejo 세조 世祖	r. 1455–1468
8. King Yejong 예종 睿宗	r. 1468–1469
9. King Seongjong 성종 成宗	r. 1469–1494
10. King Yeonsangun 연산군 燕山君	r. 1494–1506
11. King Jungjong 중종 中宗	r. 1506–1544
12. King Injong 인종 仁宗	r. 1544–1545
13. King Myeongjong 명종 明宗	r. 1545–1567
*14. King Seonjo 선조 宣祖	r. 1567–1608
*15. King Gwanghaegun 광해군 光海君	r. 1608–1623
*16. King Injo 인조 仁祖	r. 1623–1649
17. King Hyojong 효종 孝宗	r. 1649–1659
*18. King Hyeonjong 현종 顯宗	r. 1659–1674
*19. King Sukjong 숙종 肅宗	r. 1674–1720
20. King Gyeongjong 경종 景宗	r. 1720–1724
21. King Yeongjo 영조 英祖	r. 1724–1776
*22. King Jeongjo 정조 正祖	r. 1776–1800
*23. King Sunjo 순조 純祖	r. 1800–1834
24. King Heonjong 헌종 憲宗	r. 1834–1849
25. King Cheoljong 철종 哲宗	r. 1849–1863
*26. King Gojong 고종 高宗	r. 1863–1907
27. King Sunjong 순종 純宗	r. 1907–1910

(An asterisk marks each of the twelve kings who dealt with Queen Sindeok.)

Appendix 2

Children of Yi Seonggye (1335–1408)

Children by Lady Han

1. Bangu (Grand Prince Jinan) 이방우 李芳雨   1354–1393
   진안대군 鎭安大君

2. Banggwa (King Jeongjong) 이방과 李芳果   1357–1419
   Second king (r. 1399–1400) 정종 定宗

3. Bangui (Grand Prince Ikan) 이방의 李芳毅   Unknown–1404
   익안대군 益安大君

4. Banggan (Grand Prince Hoean) 이방간 李芳幹   1364–1421
   Ambitious 회안대군 懷安大君

5. Bangwon (King Taejong) 이방원 李芳遠   1367–1422
   Third king (r. 1400–1418) 태종 太宗

6. Bangyeon (Grand Prince Deokan) 이방연 李芳衍
   Unknown – unknown, died "before marrying" 덕안대군 德安大君

Daughters: Princess Gyeongsin 경신공주 慶愼公主 Unknown–1426
Princess Gyeongseon 경선공주 慶善公主 Unknwon–Unknown

Children by Lady Kang

7. Bangbeon (Grand Prince Muan) 이방번 李芳蕃 1381–1398
   Murdered in 1398 무안대군 撫安大君

8. Bangseok (Grand Prince Uian) 이방석 李芳碩 1382–1398
   Murdered in 1398 의안대군 宜安大君

Daughter: Princess Gyeongsun 경순공주 慶順公主 Unknown–1407
Married Yi Je (murdered in 1398)

Appendix 3

Relatives of Queen Sindeok

Sindeok's father and uncles

1. Yungwi 윤귀 允貴   Eldest uncle
2. Yunseong 윤성 允成   Father
3. Yunchung 윤충 允忠   Second-eldest uncle
4. Yunui 윤의 允誼   Third-eldest uncle
5. Yunhwi 윤휘 允暉   Fourth-eldest uncle
6. Yunbu 윤부 允富   Youngest uncle

Sindeok's brothers

1. Deukryong 득룡 得龍   Eldest brother
2. Sunryong 순룡 舜龍   Second-eldest brother
3. Yugwon 유권 有權   Third-eldest brother
4. Gyegwon 계권 繼權   Fourth-eldest brother

Appendix 4

Confusion over Which of Sindeok's Brothers Was the Eldest

Discrepancies in the names given for the eldest brother of Queen Sindeok were discovered long ago and are still noted in some sources today. The Kang Family Lineage Records list Deukryong as the eldest son, while Ji Doo-hwan in his study of King Taejo's family (*Taejo daewang*, 1999) lists Sunryong first. Here is the explanation from a Kang family genealogist.

Sincheon Kang-ssi daedongbo, 1979 edition preface:

Deukryong and Sunryong are sons of the Lord of Sangsan, Kang Yunseong. Since time has passed, the life stories and birth and death dates have not been too clear. Thus the Anreung branch claimed Deukryong as the first son, while the Jaeryeong branch claimed Sunryong as the first son. This disagreement could not be resolved even after analyzing many documents and records.

When we were compiling the current genealogy records, the committee agreed to abide by the oldest record, and the 1710 edition was discovered, which was in the possession of Sunryong's descendant, Kang Changgeun in [Chungcheongnam-do]. He had the 1710 edition and according to this, [Deukryong] was listed as first son. Thus we deemed this to be the authoritative ranking of the siblings, and recorded it as such.

Respectfully submitted,

Kang Jeon-mun

Appendix 5

The Official 1388 Escape Story

Two versions of this story exist. This version, taken from the *Taejo sillok prologomena* (1388), was written long after the fact, with the titles of royalty retrospectively applied (or not) and the tragic murder of the "lamented prince" mentioned, although the murder happened ten years after this story took place. It is said that this rendition shows the hostility of the court toward Queen Sindeok because everyone, even the children, are referred to as royalty except "Consort Kang."

At that time Queen Sinui (Lady Han, the primary wife) was at her estate in Pocheon, while Consort Kang lived at the Cheolhyeon (another source says Cheorwon) estate in Pocheon. His Highness was then Senior Administrator. He was in the capital when he got the news (of a certain political emergency), and rather than go to his home in the capital (which could have been dangerous), he immediately galloped off to Pocheon, only to find that his estate stewards and all the slaves had already fled.

He right away picked up the queen and the consort and headed for the northeast (Hamgyeong-do). His Highness personally put them on or let them down from the horses, and when the horses had to be fed in the stables, he attended to it. Princess Gyeongsin, Princess Gyeongseon (children of Lady Han), Grand Prince Muan, and the lamented princes (children of Lady Kang), still children at the time, were with him on this trip.

Appendix 6

Lineage of Kang Cheonik

강천익 康天翊

Kang Cheonik was a ninth descendant of Sindeok's brother Gyegwon. The royal court contacted Cheonik twice for help when planning honors for the relatives of the queen. In 1681 officials asked him to help locate the grave of her father, Yunseong, and in 1669 they went to him again to find the name of the queen's mother.

ca. 1310	Yunseong 강윤성 康允成
ca. 1345	Gyegwon 강계권 康繼權
ca. 1380	Min 강민 康 敏
ca. 1420	Chaek 강책 康 策
ca. 1460	Houi 강호의 康好義
ca. 1500	Chison 강치손 康致孫
ca. 1530	Huiwon 강희원 康熙元
ca. 1560	Yundeok 강윤덕 康潤德
ca. 1590	Gyeongham 강경함 康敬涵
ca. 1620	Yeoheup 강여흡 康汝洽
ca. 1650	Cheonik 강천익 康天翊

Appendix 7

Comparison of *Sichaek* and *Okchaek*

The two terms *sichaek* (시책 諡册) and *okchaek* (옥책 玉册) are often used as synonyms and translated as "jade book," the book that was literally made of jade, inscribed with the posthumous name of the deceased, and placed in the person's burial tomb or niche in [Jongmyo] Shrine. Various dictionaries list them as synonyms, yet in ancient Chinese law, there is a subtle difference.

Sichaek denotes the conferral of a posthumous name. According to the Korean statutes, the emperor of China conferred an honorary name upon a king or queen as part of the tributary ceremony. The *si* when used alone means "to confer," as to appoint to a paramount position or confer a title or name upon someone. The Chinese, in conferring legitimacy on the queen, used what for them was an ancient technical term known as *chaekbong* (책봉 册封). In ritual law, the act of legitimizing a person was conveyed to the recipient in the form of a *chaek*, or book, and in the case of high-ranking royalty a book made of jade in which the words conveying the enfeoffment were carved into the jade.

Thus *sichaek* literally says "confer the book" and expresses the terminology of enfeoffment in a metaphorical way. Legally, it means, "The emperor of China recognizes her as the legitimate queen of Korea," or in a more roundabout way, the emperor "conferred" (*si*) the title/honor that made her a legitimate queen and thus made it possible for her to receive the jade book (*okchaek*). Think about the sentence in English, "The judge threw the book at him." The judge did not literally throw a book. He sentenced the defendant for the violation of many different laws. In the same way, the Chinese emperor "*chaek*-ed" Lady Kang as queen.

Okchaek (jade book), on the other hand, really does refer to a book, most often one made of thin pages of jade. This reflects the high rank of the individual receiving the posthumous name; the name would be placed in the book and the book then placed in the person's ancestral temple.

The idea, then, is that the emperor of China conferred (*sichaek*-ed) the queen with legitimacy, which was then entered in the jade book (*okchaek*).

Gari Ledyard, e-mail correspondence, 2012

Appendix 8

Execution by Poison

Although there is no mention of this practice in the law codes, members of the royal family and high-ranking subjects who were condemned to death were sent a dose of poison by the king. An executioner with his entourage would come to the residence (usually a place of exile) of the condemned and announce that he had come to deliver a royal message. While the royal messenger of death waited outside, the condemned would dress himself in his court dress as if he were having a royal audience. When the condemned was ready, the messenger read the royal decree of death to the condemned and bowed before him. The poison would be made by brewing various herbs while the *ondol* in the room in which the condemned was to drink it would be heated, even during summer, so that the poison would reach the heart very quickly.

Hahm, *Korean Political Tradition and Law*, 95

NOTES

Front Matter

1. Billy Collins, *The Art of Drowning*, 3
2. Bruce Cumings, *Dominion from Sea to Sea: Pacific Ascendancy and American Power*, xvii

A Note to the Readers

1. National Institute of Korean Language, "Romanization of Korean." www.korean.go.kr/hangeul/cpron/main.htm; www.korean.go.kr/front_eng/roman/roman_01.do

Introduction

1. Kenneth Foote, *Shadowed Ground*, 62
2. David Kang, *East Asia before the West*, 57
3. Roger Janelli and Dawnhee Janelli, *Ancestor Worship and Korean Society*, 177
4. JaHyun Kim Haboush, *A Heritage of Kings*, 27
5. Bruce Cumings, *Korea's Place in the Sun*, 79
6. *Sejong sillok*, 55:6b, 1432/1/18
7. Yi Geung-ik, *Yeollyeosil gisul*, 9:50
8. David Lowenthal, *The Past Is a Foreign Country*, 192 and 215

Part One: Honor (1335–1397)

Chapter 1. The Emergence of Yi Seonggye and Lady Kang

1. Ki-baik Lee, *A New History of Korea*, 165
2. Ji Doo-hwan, *Taejo daewang*, 27 and 31
3. Peter Lee, *Sourcebook of Korean Civilization*, 1:306
4. *Goryeosa* (hereafter GRS), 35:29a–30a
5. Ibid., 38:2a
6. Ibid., 38:24b–25a
7. Ibid., 40:17b
8. Ibid., 113:29b

Chapter 2. Second Wife, Goryeo 1356–1392

1. *Jeongjo sillok*, 51:73a; 1799/6/2
2. Ji Doo-hwan, *Taejo daewang*, 191
3. *Seonwon bogam*, 3:77
4. *Hanguk minjok*, 13:699
5. GRS, 37:15b
6. Ibid., 137:18b
7. Yi Geung-ik, *Yeollyeosil*, 1:54
8. Ibid., 1:55
9. John Duncan, *The Origins of the Chosŏn Dynasty*, 180 and 184
10. GRS, 46:21b
11. Ibid., 204
12. Yi Byeong-do, *Hanguksa yeonpyo*, 351
13. *Sunjo sillok*. 27:17b, 1824/10/19
14. GRS, 46:38a and 42a
15. Peter Lee, *Sourcebook*, 1:452
16. Yi Geung-ik, *Yeollyeosil*, 1:139

17. Ji Doo-hwan, *Taejo daewang*, 35

18. GRS, 117:18a–19a

19. *Taejo sillok*, prologue 1392/4/4

20. Yi Geung-ik, *Yeollyeosil*, 1:74-75

Chapter 3. Illustrious Consort, Joseon 1392–1396

1. Yi Geung-ik, *Yeollyeosil*, 1:132

2. *Sincheon Kang-ssi sehon*, 1973, 22

3. Yi Geung-ik, *Yeollyeosil*, 1:119

4. Yi Sang tae, *Joseon yeoksa baro japgi*, 28–29

5. Yi Geung-ik, *Yeollyeosil*, 1:119

6. Seong Nak-hun, *Yijoui inmul*, 43

7. Peter Lee, *Sourcebook*, 521

8. *King Sejong the Great*, 1970, 26

9. Ji Doo-hwan, *Taejo daewang*, 92 and 168

10. *Taejo sillok*, 1:51a, 1392/8/7

11. Ibid., 2:16a, 1392/11/29

12. Kwon Yon-ung, "Seoul: Founding the New Capital." *Transactions*, 1993, 4

13. *Taejo sillok*, 1393/2/1

Chapter 4. Queen Sindeok, 1396–1397

1. *Taejo sillok*, 10:3b, 1396/8/13

2. Ibid., 10:3b–4a, 1396/8/16

3. Ibid., 10:4b, 1396/8/28

4. Ibid., 10:6a, 1396/9/28

5. *Seonwon bogam*, 3:115, 1989

6. Ji Doo-hwan, *Taejo daewang*, 169

7. Charlotte Horlyck (professor of Korean Art History at SOAS, University of London), e-mail message to author, 2010

8. Sem Vermeersch (professor of Buddhism at Seoul National University), e-mail message to author, 2010

9. *Taejo sillok*, 11:4b–8a, 1397/3/8

10. Hahm Pyong-choon, *Korean Political Tradition and Law*, 103

11. Martina Deuchler, *Confucian Transformation*, 197

12. Huang Chichung, *The Analects of Confucius*, 53

13. *Joseon wangneung*, 39 and 56

14. Son Yeong-sik, *Joseon jeilui dari*, 17–18

15. *Taejo sillok*, 10:5a, 1396/9/9

16. *Hyeonjong sillok*, 1669/1/4

17. Ibid., 1669/1/4

18. Yi Geung-ik, *Yeollyeosil*, 2

19. On-Site Temple Information Board, Heungcheonsa Temple

20. Syn Chol K., Buddhist historian, in discussion with the author, 2007

Part Two. Dishonor (1398–1450)

Chapter 5. The Chess Master

1. *King Sejong the Great*, 1970, 27

2. *Taejong sillok*, 22:13b–14a

3. Ibid., 1398/11/11

4. Ibid., 1398/12/25

5. Duncan, *Origins*, 225

6. Park Seong-rae, *Portents and Politics*, 196

7. Deuchler, *Transformation*, 143

8. Hahm Pyong-choon, *Korean Political Tradition and Law*, 117

9. *Taejong sillok*, 4:26b, 1402/12/18

Chapter 6. Four Significant Sites

1. *Taejong sillok*, 1410/7/26

2. Yi Sang-tae, *Joseon yeoksa*, 32

3. Ibid.

4. Ibid.

5. Yi Geung-ik, *Yeollyeosil*, 1:131

6. Son Yeong-sik, *Joseon jeilui dari*, 62

7. Ji Doo-hwan, *Taejo daewang*, 171

8. *Taejong sillok*, 1410/8/7

9. Sam Y. Park, *Introduction to Korean Architecture*, 2:285

10. Yi Sang-tae, *Joseon yeoksa*, 37

Chapter 7. Repairing and Appeasing

1. Ji Doo-hwan, *Taejo daewang*, 198 and 206

2. *Taejong sillok*, 4:3a, 1402/7/2

3. Buddhists often used nine-headed dragons to pray for rain, and ancient paintings of them are found even on the walls of Mogao Buddhist cave temples in Dunhuang, China, painted around 600 CE.

4. *Taejong sillok*, 31:36b–37a, 1416/5/19

5. Ibid., 31:37b, 1416/5/20

6. Deuchler, *Transformation*, 187

7. *Taejong sillok*, 32:13a–b, 1416/8/21

8. Ibid., 33:36b–37a, 1417/5i/5

9. Ibid., 33:37a, 1417/5i/5

10. Peter Lee, in Kim-Renaud, *King Sejong the Great*, 1992, 63

11. *King Sejong the Great*, 1970, 39

12. *Sejong sillok.* 86:2a, 1439/7/2

13. Ibid., 1:10a

14. Yi Hong-jik, *Guksa daesajeon*, 52

15. Deuchler, *Transformation*, 170

16. *Sejong sillok*, 55:6b, 1432/1/18

17. Insoo Cho, professor of art history at University of Southern California, e-mail message to author, May 2005

18. *Sejong sillok*, 1434/3/20

19. Ibid., 1437/6/3

20. Ji Doo-hwan, *Taejo daewang*, 198 and 204

21. Ibid., 9:25a; 1457/10/21

22. *Taejong sillok*, 1416/8/21

Part Three. Ideological Warfare (1500–1669)

Chapter 8. The Rise of the Scholar-Officials

1. D. C. Lau, *Mencius*, 117

2. Haboush, *Heritage of Kings*, 26–7

3. Keith Pratt and Richard Rutt, *Korea: A Historical and Cultural Dictionary*, 396, 169

4. Peter Lee, *Korean Storyteller's Miscellany*, 10–11

5. Kim Sung-moon, *Between Confucian Ideology*, 247

6. Deuchler, "The Practice of Confucianism," in Benjamin Elman, *Rethinking Confucianism*, 298

7. Choung Hae-chang, ed., *Confucian Philosophy*, 124

Chapter 9. A Young Man's Request

1. *Seonjo sillok*, original, 1581/10/16

2. Gari Ledyard, "Confucianism and War," *Journal of Korean Studies*, 6 (1988–89): 96–102

3. Ibid., 90

4. Yi Geung-ik, *Yeollyeosil*, 1:132

5. Ibid.

6. *Seonjo sillok*, supplement, 15:28b, 1581/11/1

7. Ji Doo-hwan, *Taejo daewang*, 172

8. Yi Geung-ik, *Yeollyeosil*, 1:132

9. Ibid.

10. Ibid., 1:137

11. *Seonjo sillok*, 15:22b, 1581/12/18

12. Ibid., 15:23a, 1581/12/24

13. Ibid., 16:1a, 1582/1/1

14. Yi Geung-ik, *Yeollyeosil*, 1:133

15. *Seonjo sillok*, 17:10b, 1583/3/25

16. Yi Geung-ik, *Yeollyeosil*, 1:133

Chapter 10. One Decade, Two Extremes

1. Pratt and Rutt, *Historical and Cultural Dictionary*, 252

2. *Gwanghaegun sillok*, 23:71b–24:7a, 1613/6/3

3. Ibid., 42:65b, 1617/11/25

4. Eight years later, in 1637, Choe (1586–1647) had risen at court to become instrumental in negotiating a peaceful settlement with the Manchus.

5. Yi Sang tae, *Joseon yeoksa*, 35

Chapter 11. Crescendo

1. For details of both devastating conflicts, covering who was involved, discussions, longevity, and implications, see Haboush and Deuchler, *Culture and State*, 46–90.
2. *Hyeonjong sillok*, 16:2a, 1669/1/4
3. Ibid.
4. *Hyeonjong sillok*, 16:3b, 1669/1/5
5. Yi Geung-ik, *Yeollyeosil*, 1:40
6. *Hyeonjong sillok*, 16:11b, 1669/1/27
7. Ibid., 16:48b, 1669/5/14
8. Ibid., 17:6b, 1669/7/13
9. Ibid., 21:27a, 1669/7/14

Chapter 12. Finally, Enshrinement

1. Enshrinement details other than those found in the manual were gathered from Chi, *Jongmyo iyagi*, 2005; *Hyeonjong sillok*, revised, 21:50a–51b, 1669/9/24–10/1; Seon Jeong-sun, *Jeongmyo uigwe*, 2008; and www.jongmyo.net/. Accessed 2008, 2010.
2. *Hyeonjong sillok*, 17:13b, 1669/8/5
3. Ibid., 17:14b, 1669/8/9
4. Ibid., 1669/8/18
5. Ibid., 21:40b, 1669/8/20
6. For a comparison of *sichaek* and *okchaek*, see Appendix 7
7. Seon Jeong sun, *Jongmyo uigwe*, 1:250, 253
8. Yi Geung-ik, *Yeollyeosil*, 9:50
9. *Hyeonjong sillok*, 21:45a, 1669/9/3
10. Ji Doo-hwan, *Taejo daewang*, 181
11. *Sindeok wanghu bumyo dogam uigwe*, 146B–153A
12. *Hyeonjong sillok*, 21:51a, 1669/9/28

13. Comment by research assistant at Gyujanggak, 2002

14. www.jongmyo.net, Accessed 2008, 2010.

15. *Hyeonjong sillok*, 1669/10/1

Part Four: A Name Remembered (1674–2005)

Chapter 13. From Honor to Honors

1. *Sukjong sillok*, 4:45a, 1675/9/18

2. See Appendix 8 on the royal use of poison

3. *Sukjong sillok*, 9:71b, 1680/7/27

4. Ibid., 12:4a, 1681/7/23

5. Ibid., 11:53a, 1681/5/27

6. For Kang Cheonik's lineage, see Appendix 6

7. *Sukjong sillok*, 12:31b, 1681/10/16

8. Ibid., 14:8b, 1683/6/3

9. Ibid., 43:18a, 1699/5/13

10. Yi Tae-jin, "King Chongjo," in *Korea Journal* 40:4 Winter 2000, 171

11. *Jeongjo sillok*, 33:74a, 1791/12/8

12. Ibid., 42:40b, 1795/2i/20

13. Ibid., 51:73a, 1799/6/2

14. *Sunjo sillok*, 7:8a, 1805/2/4

15. Ibid., 27:9a, 1824/7/22

16. Ibid., 27:17b, 1824/10/19

Chapter 14. Into the Twentieth Century

1. *Gojong sillok*, 40:59a, 1900/6/19
2. Lowenthal, *The Past*, 57
3. Robert Buswell, *Zen Monastic Experience*, 40–41
4. *Neung jehyang gyojae* (Royal Tomb Incense Ritual Manual)

Chapter 15. Tombstones without a Tomb

1. Son, *Joseon jeilui dari*, 17
2. Isabel Bishop, *Korea and Her Neighbors*, 45
3. Son, *Joseon jeilui dari*, 16
4. Foote, *Shadowed Ground*, 28
5. *JoongAng Ilbo*, August 20, 1994

GLOSSARY

* For kings of Joseon, see Appendix 1
* For children of Yi Seonggye, see Appendix 2

akcha 악차 幄次

Anbyeon 안변 安邊

Bak Jonghun 박종훈 朴宗薰

banhon (mourning ritual) 반혼 返魂

biseok (stele or monument) 비석 碑石

Bongsangsi 봉상시 奉常寺

bonneung (royal tomb) 본릉 本陵

Mount Putuo Isalnd 보타낙가산 普陀
落伽山

bugyori (junior fifth councillor) 부교리
副校理

bujehak (first counselor) 부제학 副提學

Bupyeong 부평 富平

busuchan (junior sixth counselor)
부수찬 副修撰

Byeon Gyeryang 변계량 卞季良

Byeongjo (Board of War) 병조 兵曹

Chae Jeunggwang 채증광 蔡增光

Cheolhyeon 철현 鐵峴

Cheonggyecheon Stream
청계천 淸溪川

Cheorwon 철원 鐵原

Choe Myeonggil 최명길 崔鳴吉

Choe Yeong 최영 崔瑩

Chunchugwan (State Archives) 춘추관
春秋館

Chwihyeonbang 취현방 聚賢坊

Daedong Jongyakwon (Jeonju Yi
[Lee] Royal Family Association)
대동종약원 大同宗約院

Deogwon 덕원 德源

Deokcheon 덕천 德川

Euphwadang Hall 읍화당 挹華堂

Gaepung-gun 개풍군 開豊郡

Gangnyeongjeon Hall 강녕전 康寧殿

Geonwonneung Royal Tomb 건원릉
健元陵

geumbo (royal seal)
금보 金寶

gokjang 곡장 曲墻

Gokju 곡주 谷州

Goksan 곡산 谷山

Gongjo (Board of Works) 공조 工曹

gwageo (civil examination) 과거 科擧

Gwangmyeongsa Temple
광명사 廣明寺

Gwangpyeong, Grand Prince 광평대군
廣平大君

Gwangtonggyo Bridge 광통교 廣通橋

Gwon Geun 권근 權近

gyemo (stepmother) 계모 繼母

Gyeongan 경안 慶安

Gyeongcheonsa Temple 경천사 敬天寺

Hamheung 함흥 咸興

Han Cheolje 한철제 韓喆濟

Han Chung 한충 韓忠

Han Jangseok 한장석 韓章錫

Han, Lady 한비 韓妃

Hansik 한식 寒食

Heo Jeok 허적 許積

Heo Mok 허목 許穆

Heungcheonsa Temple 흥천사 興天寺

Hojo (Board of Revenue) 호조 戶曹

Hongwu, Emperor (China) 홍무제 洪武帝

Hongmungwan (Office of Special Counselors) 홍문관 弘文館

Hwang Hui 황희 黃喜

Hwanjo Daewang (Great King Hwanjo, honoring of Yi Jachun) 환조대왕 桓祖大王

hwasang (portrait) 화상 畫像

Hyeonbi 현비 顯妃

Hyoso 효소 孝昭

Icheon 이천 利川

Inanjeon Hall 인안전 仁安殿

Jaebyeok-dong 재벽동 滓璧洞

jehyang 제향 祭享

jemun 제문 祭文

Jeolbi 절비 節妃

Jeollye gyoyuk yeonsu gyojae (Manual for Learning the Rituals at Jongmyo Shrine) 전례교육연수교재 典禮教育研修教材

Jeong Dojeon 정도전 鄭道傳

Jeong Huigye 정희계 鄭熙啓

Jeong Mongju 정몽주 鄭夢周

Jeong Taehwa 정태화 鄭太和

jeongbae (legitimate wife) 정배 正配

jeongjagak (T-shaped wooden ritual hall) 정자각 丁字閣

Jeongneung Royal Tomb 정릉 貞陵

Jeonju Yi 전주 이 全州李

Jereung Royal Tomb 제릉 齊陵

Jo Jun 조준 趙浚

Jo Saui 조사의 趙思義

Jongmyo Shrine 종묘 宗廟

Junggeoncheong (Board of Restoration) 중건청 重建廳

Kang Cheonik 강천익 康天翊

Kang Eun 강은 姜誾

Kang Sunil 강순일 康純一

Kang U 강우 康祐

Kang Yeong 강영 康榮

Kim Sahyeong 김사형 金士衡

Kim Suhang 김수항 金壽恒

Gyujanggak Royal Library 규장각 奎章閣

Maengsan 맹산 孟山

munseok (tomb statues) 문석 文石

myo (tomb of—) 묘 墓

Nam Eun 남은 南誾

Namin (Southern Faction) 남인 南人

neung (royal tomb) 능 陵

Neung jehyang gyojae (Royal Tomb Incense Ritual Manual Tomb) 능제향교재 陵祭享教材

Nosan, Prince 노산군 魯山君

okchaek (jade book) 옥책 玉册

Pocheon 포천 抱川

Saganwon (Censor-General) 사간원 司諫院

Saheonbu (Office of Inspector

General) 사헌부 司憲府

Samsa (Three Boards) 삼사 三司

Sangsan 상산 象山

sarijeon 사리전 舍利殿

Seo Yeongbo 서영보 徐榮輔

Seoin (Western Faction) 서인 西人

seongmul 석물 石物

Seonjeongjeon Hall 선정전 宣政殿

Seonjukgyo Bridge 선죽교 善竹橋

sichaek (epitaph book) 시책 諡冊

sidokgwan (reader) 시독관 侍讀館

siho (posthumous name) 시호 諡號

sillo (a type of shaman ritual)
  신로 神路

Sillyusan Mountain 신류산 神留山

Sim Hyosaeng 심효생 沈孝生

Sinheungam Hermitage 신흥암 新興庵

Sinheungsa Temple 신흥사 新興寺

sinjangseok 신장석 神將石

sinju 신주 神主

Sinui, Queen 신의왕후 神懿王后

Song Siyeol 송시열 宋時烈

Soreung Royal Tomb 소릉 昭陵

Suchangmun Gate 수창문 壽昌門

Sunwon hyeongyeong
  순원현경 順元顯敬

Suridogam deungnok (Registry
  of the Superindent of Repairs)
  수리도감등록 修理都監登錄

Tongnyewon (Comprehensive Rites
  Agency) 통례원 通禮院

Tushan, Lady (China) 도산비 塗山妃

Uijeongbu (State Council)
  의정부 議政府

Uiryesangjeongso (Office for the
  Establishment of Ceremonies)
  의례상정소 儀禮詳定所

wipae (spirit tablets) 위패 位牌

wondeok 원덕 元德

Yejo (Board of Rites) 예조 禮曹

Yeo Uison 여의손 呂義孫

Yeollyeosil gisul (Narrative of
  Yeollyeosil) 연려실기술 燃藜室記述

Yeongheung 영흥 永興

yeongjeong 영정 影幀

Yi Chang 이창 李昌

Yi Deukbun 이득분 李得芬

Yi Geung-ik 이긍익 李肯翊

Yi Je 이제 李濟

Yi Mansu 이만수 李晩秀

Yi Saek 이색 李穡

Yi Uigeon 이의건 李義建

Yongbong (Dragon Peak) 용봉 龍峰

Yongyeon (Dragon Pond) 용연 龍淵

Yun Hyu 윤휴 尹鑴

Youshen, Lady (China) 유신비 有莘妃

BIBLIOGRAPHY

Baker, Donald. "Factionalism in Perspective: Causes and Consequences of Political Struggles during the Choson Dynasty." *Korean Studies in Canada*, 1994, 2–10.

Bishop, Isabella. *Korea and Her Neighbors*. Seoul: Yonsei University Press, 1970.

Buswell, Robert. *The Zen Monastic Experience*. Princeton: Princeton University Press, 1992.

Chae Gil. *In Treasures*. San Francisco: Asian Art Museum, Fall 2003: 7:1.

Collins, Billy. *The Art of Drowning*. University of Pittsburgh Press, 1995.

Choung, Haechang, ed. *Confucian Philosophy in Korea*. Seongnam, Korea: The Academy of Korean Studies, 1996.

Chung, Man-jo. "The Political Program of the Sallim Faction (Sandang) in the Mid-Seventeenth Century." In *Korean Studies: New Pacific Currents*, edited by Dae-sook Suh, Honolulu: University of Hawaii, Center for Korean Studies, 1994, 29–40.

Chung, Chai-shik. "Chǒng Tojǒn: Architect of Yi Dynasty Government and Ideology." In *Rise of Neo-Confucianism in Korea*, edited by Wm. Theodore de Bary and JaHyun Kim Haboush, New York: Columbia University Press, 1985.

Chung, Edward. *The Korean Neo-Confucianism of Yi T'oegye and Yi Yulgok*. Albany: State University of New York Press, 1995.

Cumings, Bruce. *Korea's Place in the Sun*. New York: Norton & Co., 1997.

Cumings, Bruce. *Dominion from Sea to Sea: Pacific Ascendancy and American Power*. New Haven: Yale University Press, 2010.

De Bary, William Theodore and JaHyun Kim Haboush, eds. *Rise of Neo-Confucianism in Korea*. New York: Columbia University Press, 1985.

Deuchler, Martina. *Confucian Transformation of Korea*. Cambridge: Harvard University Press, 1992.

Deuchler, Martina. "Propagating Female Virtue." In *Women and Confucian Cultures*, edited by Dorothy Ko and JaHyun Kim Haboush, Berkeley: University of California Press, 2003.

Duncan, John. "Confucianism in the Later Koryŏ and Early Chosŏn," In *Korean Studies* 18 (1994): 76–102.

Duncan, John. *The Origins of the Chosŏn Dynasty*. Seattle: University of Washington Press, 2000.

Elman, Benjamin, John Duncan, and Herman Ooms, eds. *Rethinking Confucianism Past and Present in China, Japan, Korea and Vietnam*. Los Angeles: University of California at Los Angeles, 2002.

Foote, Kenneth. *Shadowed Ground: America's Landscapes of Violence and Tragedy*. Austin: University of Texas Press, 1997.

Gersi, Douchan. *Faces in the Smoke*. Los Angeles: Jeremy Tarcher, 1991.

Goryeosa [Annals of the Goryeo Dynasty]. Yonhui Daehakgyo Dongbanghak Yeonguso, 1955.

Government-General of Joseon. *Chosen shi*. Part iv, vol. 1, Seoul: Government-General of Joseon, 1932, 125

Gukjo mungwa bangmok [Register of Civil Examination]. Seoul: Taehaksa, 1984.

Gukjo bangmok. [Register of Civil Examination]. Seoul: National Assembly Library, 1971.

Guide to the National Folk Museum. Seoul: National Folk Museum, 1994.

Haboush, JaHyun Kim. "Education of Yi Crown Prince." In *Rise of Neo-Confucianism in Korea*, edited by Wm. Theodore de Bary, New York: Columbia University Press, 1985.

Haboush, JaHyun Kim. "Confucian Rhetoric and Ritual as Technique of Political Dominance." *Journal of Korean Studies* 5 (1987): 39–62.

Haboush, JaHyun Kim. *A Heritage of Kings: One Man's Monarchy in the Confucian World.* New York: Columbia University Press, 1988.

Haboush, JaHyun Kim & Martina Deuchler. *Culture and the State in Late Chosŏn.* Cambridge: Harvard Asia Center, 1999.

Haboush, JaHyun Kim, ed. *Epistolary Korea: Letters in the Communicative Space of the Chosŏn, 1392–1910.* New York: Columbia University Press, 2009.

Hahm, Pyong-choon. *Korean Political Tradition and Law.* Seoul: Royal Asiatic Society, 1987.

Hanguk Jeongsin Munhwa Yeonguwon. *Hanguk minjok munhwa daebaekgwa sajeon* [Great Encyclopedia of Korean People and Culture], vol. 13. Seoul: Hanguk Jeongsin Munhwa Yeonguwon, 1991

Han, Woo-keun. *The History of Korea.* Honolulu: East-West Center Press, 1971.

Henthorn, William. *Korea: The Mongol Invasions.* Leiden: E.J. Brill, 1963.

Heungcheonsa Temple. english.seongbuk.go.kr/travel/culturalassets.htm/. Accessed 2008.

Horlyck, Charlotte. "Confucian Burial Practices in the Late Goryeo and Early Joseon Periods." *The Review of Korean Studies* 11.2 (2008): 33–58.

Huang, Chichung. *The Analects of Confucius.* Oxford University Press, 1997.

Hyeonjong sillok [Annals of King Hyeonjong]. Seoul: Minjok Munhwa Yeonguhoe, 1992.

Institute of the Translation of Korean Classics. *Jongmyo uigwe* [Jongmyo Rituals]. vol. 1 and 2, Translated by Seon, Jeong sun. Seoul: , Gimm-Young Publishers, 2008.

Im, Donggweon. *Hanil gungjunguirye ui yeongu* [Study of Court Rituals of Korea]. Seoul: Chungang University Press, 1995.

Im Jungung. *Wangbi yeoljeon* [Chronicles of the Queens]. Seoul: Korea Sun-Young Publishing Co., 2003.

Janelli, Roger, and Dawnhee Janelli. *Ancestor Worship and Korean Society.*

Stanford: Stanford University Press, 1982.

Jeollye gyoyuk yeonsu gyojae [Instruction Manual for Rituals at Jongmyo]. Seoul: Jongmyo Jerye Bojonhoe (Jeonju Yi Clan Headquarters, Jongmyo Shrine Ceremony Preservation Commission), 2002.

Jeongneung Royal Tomb. Site brochure. Seoul, Korea.

Jeongneung sajeok [Jeongneung Royal Tomb Historical Landmark]. Seoul: Cultural Heritage Administration.

Ji Doo-hwan. *Gwanghaegungwa chinincheok* [Prince Gwanghae and His Relatives]. Seoul: Yeoksa Munhwa, 2002.

Ji Doo-hwan. *Hyeonjong daewanggwa chinincheok* [Great King Hyeonjong and His Relatives]. Seoul: Yeoksa Munhwa, 2009.

Ji Doo-hwan. *Jeongjong daewanggwa chinincheok* [Great King Jeongjong and His Relatives]. Seoul: Yeoksa Munhwa, 1999.

Ji Doo-hwan. *Jongmyo iyagi; segye munhwa yusan* [The Story of Jongmyo Shrine: Cultural Heritage of the World]. Paju, Korea: Jipmundang, 2005.

Ji Doo-hwan. *Seonjo daewanggwa chinincheok* [Great King Seonjo and His Relatives]. Seoul: Yeoksa Munhwa, 2002.

Ji Doo-hwan. *Taejo daewanggwa chinincheok* [Great King Taejo and His Relatives]. Seoul: Yeoksa Munhwa, 1999.

Jongmyojerye. Jeonju Yi [Lee] Royal Family Association, www.jongmyo.net. Accessed 2008.

Joseon wangjo sillok (*Annals of the Joseon Dynasty*). National Institute of Korean History, sillok.history.go.kr/. Accessed 2008.

Joseon wangjo sillok [Annals of the Joseon Dynasty]. Seoul: Minjok Munhwa Chujinhoe, 1955.

Joseon wangneung [Royal tombs of Joseon]. Seoul: Cultural Properties Administration, 1986.

Kalton, Michael. "Early Yi Dynasty Neo-Confucianism: An Integrated Vision."

In *Religion and Ritual in Korean Society*, edited by Laura Kendall, and Griffin Dix, Berkeley: Institute of East Asian Studies, 1987.

Kang, David. *East Asia before the West: Five Centuries of Trade and Tribute*. New York: Columbia University Press, 2010.

Kang, Hildi. *Family Lineage Records as a Resource for Korean History: A Case Study of Thirty-Nine Generations of the Sinchŏn Kang Family*. Lewiston: The Edwin Mellen Press, 2007

Kang, Su-won. *Hanguk inmyeong sajeon* [Korean Biographical Dictionary]. Seoul: Ilsinsa, 1959.

Kendall, Laura and Griffin Dix, eds. *Religion and Ritual in Korean Society*. Berkeley: Institute of East Asian Studies, University of California, 1987.

Keum, Jang-tae. *Confucianism and Korean Thoughts*. Seoul: Jimoondang Publishing Co., 2000.

Kim, Gyeong-hui. "*Korea ro bullida*." In *Goryeo sidae saramdeul iyagi* (*Stories of Goryeo Dynasty People*), edited by Yongun Pak et al., vol. 2, Seoul: Sinseowon, 2001, 155–163.

Kim, Kumja Paik. *Goryeo Dynasty, Korea's Age of Enlightenment, 918–1392*. San Francisco: Asian Art Museum, 2003.

Kim, Sanggi. *Goryeo sidae-sa* [History of Goryeo]. Seoul: Seoul University Press, 1985.

Kim, Sung Moon. "Between Confucian Ideology and the State: A New Approach in Understanding the Literati Purge of 1519." *The Review of Korean Studies* 5.2 (2002): 233–260.

Kim, Sun Joo, and Jungwon Kim. *Wrongful Deaths: Selected Inquest Records from Nineteenth-Century Korea*. Seattle: University of Washington Press, 2014.

Kim-Renaud, Young-Key, ed. *King Sejong the Great*. Washington, DC: International Circle of Korean Language, 1992.

King Sejong the Great. Seoul: King Sejong Memorial Society (Sejong Daewang

Ginyeom Saephoe), 1970.

Ko, Dorothy, JaHyun Kim Haboush, and Joan Piggott. *Women and Confucian Cultures in Premodern China, Korea and Japan.* Berkeley: University of California Press, 2003.

Korean Ancient Palaces. Seoul: Youl Hwa Dang Publishing Co., 1988.

"Korean learning for correct pronunciation." National Institute of Korean Language, www.korean.go.kr/hangeul/cpron/main.htm. Accessed 2008.

Kwon, Yon-ung. "Seoul: Founding the New Capital." In *Transactions*, Seoul: Royal Asiatic Society, 1993.

Lankov, Andrei. "Controversy over Ritual in 17th Century Korea." *Seoul Journal of Korean Studies* 3 (1990): 49–64.

Lau, D.C. *Mencius.* New York: Penguin Books, 1970.

Ledyard, Gari. "Confucianism and War: The Korean Security Crisis of 1598." *Journal of Korean Studies* 6 (1988–89): 81–119.

Lee, Ki-baik. *A New History of Korea.* Cambridge: Harvard University Press, 1984.

Lee, Peter. *Korean Storyteller's Miscellany.* Princeton: Princeton University Press, 1989.

Lee, Peter, ed. *Sourcebook of Korean Civilization.* vol. 1, New York: Columbia University Press, 1993.

Lee, Peter, ed. *Sourcebook of Korean Civilization.* vol. 2, New York: Columbia University Press, 1996.

Lee, Seong-mu. "On the Causes of Factional Strife in Late Chosŏn." *Korean Studies: New Pacific Currents*, edited by Dae-sook Suh, Honolulu: University of Hawaii, Center for Korean Studies, 1994, 3–28.

Lewis, Bernard. *History: Remembered, Recovered, Invented.* Princeton: Princeton University Press, 1975.

Lowenthal, David. *The Past Is a Foreign Country.* Cambridge: Cambridge

University Press, 1985.

Lukacs, John. *Historical Consciousness, or the Remembered Past*. New York: Harper & Row, 1968.

Nahm, Andrew. *Korea: Tradition and Transformation*. Elizabeth, New Jersey: Hollym, 1988.

Neung jehyang gyojae [Manual for Royal Tomb Ceremonies]. Courtesy of Yi Sam-mok, Clan Official. Seoul: Protocol Office, Jeonju Yi [Lee] Royal Family Association (private publication).

O, Hui-bok. *Bonggeon gwanryo gigu mit byeoseul ireum pyeonram* [Manual of Organizations and Ranks during the Feudal Periods]. Seoul: Yeogang chulpansa, 1992.

Oh, Yeongseon. "Living in Goryeo, Land of Tolerance." In *Goryeo saenghwalgwan 1* [Goryeo Lifestlye 1]. Hanguk saenghwalsa bakmulgwan [The Museum of Everyday Life through Korean History] vol. 7. Paju, Korea: Sakyejul, 2002.

Pak, Jonggi. *O baek nyeon Goryeosa* [Five Hundred Years of Goryeo History]. Seoul: Pureun Yeoksa, 1999.

Pak, Yong-un. *Goryeo sidae saramdul iyagi* [Stories of People in Goryeo Period]. Seoul: Sin Seowon, 2003.

Palais, James. "Confucianism and the Aristocratic/Bureaucratic Balance in Korea." *Harvard Journal of Asiatic Studies* 44.2 (1984): 427–468.

Paludan, Ann. *Chronicles of the Chinese Emperors*. London: Thames and Hudson Ltd., 1998.

Park, Sam. *An Introduction to Korean Architecture*. Seoul: Jungwoo-sa Publishing Co., 1991.

Park, Seong-Rae. *Portents and Politics in Korean History*. Seoul: Jimoondang Publishing Company, 1998.

Pratt, Keith and Richard Rutt. *Korea: A Historical and Cultural Dictionary.*

Surrey: Curzon Press, 1999.

Rogers, Michael. "P'yŏnnyŏn T'ongnok: The Foundation Legend of the Koryŏ State." *The Journal of Korean Studies* 4 (1982–83): 3–70.

"Romanization of Korean." National Institute of Korean Language, www.korean. go.kr/front_eng/roman/roman_01.do. Accessed 2008.

Rossabi, Morris. *The Jurchens in Yuan and Ming*. Ithaca: Cornell University Press, 1982.

Rozman, Gilbert, ed. *Confucian Heritage and Its Modern Adaptation*. Princeton: Princeton University Press, 1991.

Saebaekgwa sajeon [Dong-a's New Encyclopedia]. Seoul: Dong-a Publishing, 1959.

Setton, Mark. "Factional Politics and Philosophical Development in the Late Chosŏn." *Journal of Korean Studies* 8 (1992): 37–80.

Seong, Nak-hun. *Yijoui inmul* [Yi Dynasty's Prominent People]. vol.1–3, Seoul: Yangudang, 1988.

Seonjo sujeong sillok, 11–19 nyeon [Annals of King Seonjo (revised), years 11–19]. Seoul: Minjok Munhwa Chujinhoe, 1989.

Seongjong sillok [Annals of King Seongjong]. Seoul: King Sejong Memorial Society (Sejong Daewang Ginyeom Saephoe), 1981.

Seong-ssiui gohyang [Encyclopedia of Korean Clan Names]. Seoul: JoongAng Ilbo, 1989.

Seonwon bogam: Joseon wangjo 600 nyeon Jeonsa [Comprehensive History of the 600 Years of Joseon Dynasty]. Compiled by Jeonju Yi Clan Preservation Committee, vol.1–3, Seoul: Gyemyeongsa, 1989.

Seoul Metropolitan Government. "Cultural Significance of Gwanggyo Bridge." *Cheongyecheon Restoration Project Report*, Seoul: Seoul Metropolitna Government, 2002.

Seoul Metropolitan Government. *Back to A Future: Cheong Gye Cheon*

Restoration Project. Seoul: Seoul Metropolitan Government, 2005.

Seoul Metropolitan Government. *Seoul, Her History and Culture*. Seoul: Seoul Metropolitan Government, 1992.

Shaw, William. *Legal Norms in a Confucian State*. Berkeley: University of California Press, 1981.

Shultz, Edward. *Generals and Scholars: Military Rule in Medieval Korea*. Honolulu: University of Hawaii Press, 2000.

Sin, Myeong-Ho. *Joseonui wang* [Joseon's Kings]. Seoul: Garam Books, 1998.

Sincheon Kang-ssi daedongbo [Comprehensive Lineage of Sincheon Kang]. Seoul: Sincheon Kang Clan Association, 1979.

Sincheon Kang-ssi sehon [Kang Clan Lineage Record Excerpts]. Seoul: Sincheon Kang Clan Association, 1973.

Sindeok wanghu bumyo dogam uigwe [Manual of Superintendency for the Transfer of the Spirit Tablet of Queen Sindeok to Jongmyo]. Taebaeksan Mountain History Archive, Seoul, 1669.

Son, Yeong-sik. *Joseon jeilui dari Gwangtong-gyo* [The Number One Bridge in the Joseon Period, the Gwangtonggyo Bridge]. Seoul: Chohung Bank, 1994.

Song, Kimberly. "Splash of the Past." Far Eastern Economic Review, January, 2004.

Sumiyabaatar (Seo Midal). *Jungse han-mong gwangyesa: munheonpyeon*. [(History of Mid-Goryeo–Mongol Relations]. Seoul: Dankook University Press, 1992.

Vermeersch, Sem. *The Power of the Buddhas: The Politics of Buddhism During the Goryeo Dynasty (918–1392)*. Harvard University Asia Center, 2008.

Wagner, Edward. *The Literati Purges: Political Conflict in Early Yi Korea*. Cambridge: East Asian Research Center, Harvard University, 1974.

Yang, Key P., and Gregory Henderson. "An Outline History of Korean Confucianism, Part II: The Schools of Yi Confucianism." *Journal of Asian*

Studies 18.2 (1959): 259–276.

Yi, Byeong-do. *Hanguksa yeonpyo* [History of Korea, Chronological Tables].
Seoul: Chintan Society, Eulyoo Publishing, 1959.

Yi, Byeong-do. *Hanguksa daegwan* [Overview of Korean History]. Seoul:
Bomungak, 1968.

Yi, Geunho. *Joseon wangjosa* [History of Joseon Kings]. Paju, Korea: Chunga
Book, 2005.

Yi, Geung-ik. *Yeollyeosil gisul.* [Narratives of Yellyeosil]. Translated by Yi
Byeong-do. Seoul: Minjok Munhwa Chujinhoe, 1966.

Yi, Hongjik, ed, *Guksa daesajeon* [Encyclopedia of Korean History]. Seoul:
Kyohaksa, 2002.

Choe, Beomseo. *Iyagi Goryeo wangjo-sa.* [Stories of the Goryeo Kings]. Edited
by Hyeonhui Yi. Seoul: Chunga Book, 1996.

Yi, Jae-Hwang, trans. *Taejo Jeongjong bongi* [Taejo and Jeongjong Veritable
Records, Selected Passages]. Seoul: Cheonggan Media, 2001.

Yi Sang-Tae. *Joseon yeoksa baro japgi* [History of Joseon: Correcting
Misunderstandings]. Seoul: Garam Books, 2000.

Yi, Seongmu. *Joseon wangjo sillok eoddeon chaek inga* [Joseon Dynasty Records,
What Kind of Book Is It?]. Seoul: Dongbang Media, 1999.

Yi, Tae-Jin. "King Chongjo: Confucianism, Enlightenment, and Absolute Rule."
Korea Journal 40.4 (2000): 168–201.

Yi, Yanggi. *Joseon wangjosa* [History of the Joseon Dynasty]. Seoul: Chunga
Book, 2005.

Yu, Jae-Ha, ed. *Goryeo wangjo-sa* [History of Goryeo Dynasty, vol. 5–6]. Seoul:
Hakmun Publishing, 2000.

Yun, Jeong-ran. *Joseonui wangbi* [Queens of the Joseon Dynasty]. Seoul: Charim,
1999.

INDEX

Credits

Writer	Hildi Kang
Publisher	Kim Hyunggeun
Editor	Park Jiyoung
Copy Editors	Anna Bloom, Eileen Cahill
Designer	Jung Hyun-young

photographs

Chohung Bank 187 (top)
Gyujanggak Library of Seoul National University 154, 155
Hildi Kang 74 (top), 162
LACMA collections (www.lacma.org) 114
National Cultural Heritage Research Institute, Korea 72, 94 (bottom)
Seoul Selection 18 (top), 97 (top), 176, 187 (bottom)
Steven Kang 97 (bottom)
www.art-and-archaeology.com 110
Yonhap Photo 18 (bottom), 34, 74 (bottom), 75, 94 (top), 158